UNLOCKING SHAKESPEARE'S LANGUAGE

UNLOCKING SHAKESPEARE'S LANGUAGE

HELP FOR THE TEACHER AND STUDENT

RANDAL ROBINSON

Michigan State University

National Council of Teachers of English
ERIC Clearinghouse on Reading and Communication Skills

For Marella—

Staff Editor: Robert A. Heister

Cover Design: Michael J. Getz

Interior Book Design: Tom Kovacs for TGK Design

NCTE Stock Number 55685

Published 1988 by the ERIC Clearinghouse on Reading and Communication Skills and the National Council of Teachers of English, 1111 Kenyon Road, Urbana, Illinois 61801. Printed in the United States of America.

This publication was prepared with funding from the Office of Educational Research and Improvement, U.S. Department of Education, under contract no. 400-86-0045. Contractors undertaking such projects under government sponsorship are encouraged to express freely their judgment in professional and technical matters. Prior to publication, the manuscript was submitted to the Editorial Board of the National Council of Teachers of English for critical review and determination of professional competence. This publication has met such standards. Points of view or opinions, however, do not necessarily represent the official view or opinions of either the National Council of Teachers of English or the Office of Educational Research and Improvement.

Library of Congress Cataloging-in-Publication Data

Robinson, Randal F., 1936–
    Unlocking Shakespeare's language: help for the teacher and student / Randal Robinson.
        p.   cm. — (Theory & research into practice)
    Bibliography: p.
    ISBN 0-8141-5568-5
    1. Shakespeare, William, 1564–1616—Study and teaching.
  2. Shakespeare, William, 1564–1616—Language.   I. Title.
  II. Series.
PR2987.R6 1989
822.3'3—dc19

                                          88-18053
                                            CIP

CONTENTS

FOREWORD

This book was developed during the time period when the ERIC Clearinghouse on Reading and Communication Skills (ERIC/RCS) was sponsored by the National Council of Teachers of English. The Educational Resources Information Center (ERIC) is a national information system developed by the U.S. Department of Education and sponsored by the Office of Educational Research and Improvement (OERI). ERIC provides ready access to descriptions of exemplary programs, research and development reports, and related information useful in developing effective educational programs.

Through its network of specialized centers or clearinghouses, each of which is responsible for a particular educational area, ERIC acquires, evaluates, abstracts, and indexes current significant information and lists this information in its reference publications.

The ERIC system has already made available—through the ERIC Document Reproduction Service—a considerable body of data, including all federally funded research reports since 1956. However, if the findings of specific educational research are to be used by teachers, much of the data must be translated into an essentially different context. Rather than resting at the point of making research reports readily accessible, OERI has directed the ERIC clearinghouses to commission authorities in various fields to write information analysis papers.

This book, then, is the most recent of dozens of practitioner-oriented texts developed by ERIC/RCS under the sponsorship of NCTE, 1972–1987. The Clearinghouse and the Council hope that the materials are helpful in clarifying important educational issues and in improving classroom practice.

Charles Suhor
Deputy Executive Director, NCTE

1 THEORY AND RESEARCH

SHAKESPEARE'S LANGUAGE IN THE HIGH SCHOOL AND UNDERGRADUATE CLASSROOM

Dramatic works by William Shakespeare became popular as school texts toward the end of the nineteenth century. In that period, as Homer Swander points out, the English-speaking nations were moving "more fully into systems of universal education" and educators wanted classics composed in English to replace "the classics in Greek and Latin that had served well enough in more aristocratic times" (1985, 875). Yet, as teachers everywhere know, the Shakespearean English that these nineteenth-century educators selected to replace the Latin of Virgil and the Greek of Homer is itself no easy language for students. As the product of a period removed nearly four hundred years from our own, the English of Shakespeare's dramatic characters seems somewhat foreign to us in both content and idiom. Further, as the creation of a playwright who possessed exceptional goals and talents, Shakespeare's dramatic language also seems somewhat foreign to us in manner and style. It is, first of all, an English for performers, not for general readers: an English directed by a playwright to a group of fellow actors who could interpret and finish his scripts in what he called a "theater" and a "playhouse"—a seeing and a pretending place. Second, it is an English used often to form a special kind of discourse—a poetic, blank verse discourse—that is animated and governed in part by rhythmical considerations. Finally, it is an English that frequently manifests its shaper's intelligence, ingenuity, and daring in being highly compressed and elliptical and, thus, in asking a superb concentration of us all.

In fact, so far from easy is Shakespeare's dramatic language—so different from the English of our students' homes and playgrounds—that only the rarest of teachers can claim to have no significant problems with it in the classroom. When struggling with a Shakespearean text, our students frequently have trouble making out its "prose sense"—to borrow some phrases from I. A. Richards—"its plain, overt meaning, as a set of ordinary, intelligible, English sentences . . ." (1929, 12). Consequently, many students come to believe themselves incapable of ever reading Shakespeare's plays well, and thus, being discouraged, they demand that Shakespeare's works be removed from the curriculum; or else they look eagerly for summaries, paraphrases, condensations, modernized editions, and comic-book versions that they can substitute for the true Shakespearean texts.

Such attitudes from students have their impact on teachers and publishers alike, many of whom respond by recommending materials or actions that will relieve students of some or all of the burdens imposed by Shakespeare's language. Among the teachers, for example, Abraham Blinderman (1975/76) suggests that we simply drop Shakespeare's plays from all but special classes in secondary schools and junior colleges. Richard Eastman (1982) recommends that we provide partially translated versions of the plays, and Ben Renz (1942) recommends versions that are not only partially translated but also condensed. Michael McKenna (1975/76) recommends versions that mix summaries and commentaries with quotations, and Peter Thorpe (1967) argues that we should simply use much of our time in the classroom to develop translations of selected passages for our students.

As for publishers, they produce many of the very substitutes that students look for when they feel pushed either to save face or to save time. A stroll through a well-stocked bookshop or library shows, for example, a comic-book *Othello* published by Sidgwick and Jackson; a scene-by-scene summary of *King Lear* in the persistently popular series known as Cliffs Notes; a line-by-line paraphrase of *Macbeth* prepared by Alan Durband for Hutchinson's Shakespeare Made Easy Series; a slightly altered (and heavily publicized) *Hamlet* prepared by A. L. Rowse for the Contemporary Shakespeare Series of University Press of America; and a shortened *As You Like It*, with bits of paraphrase and commentary and with statements about movement inserted to accompany the dialogue, prepared by Diane Davidson for Swan's Shakespeare on Stage Series. Although such offerings, at best, condescend to students and, at worst, promise much and deliver little (see, for example, points made about Rowse's work by Feingold 1984), and although all try to simplify what "cannot be 'easy' and still be Shakespeare" (Editorial, 1985, 6), their appeal remains strong. Students simply have trouble conceiving of, or finding, works that are more immediately helpful.

Nonetheless, students really do want works better than these. They want, and need, materials that will help them understand the lines of Shakespeare's passionate and difficult dramas in the most basic of ways; materials that will enable them to increase their powers as readers and to cast out intermediaries; materials that will prepare them to explore Shakespeare's language in theatrical exercises and to use that language to express themselves, intensely and dramatically, as performers. And because students really want these materials, teachers need to conduct research to find out exactly what those materials are, and they need to do so by paying close attention to the habits, attitudes, and deficiencies of the students themselves. Only through such research can we isolate those practices of Shakespearean characters that most frequently trouble students, and only through such research can we develop approaches that are suitable for the presentation of Shakespeare's language in the modern classroom. As Gladys Veidemanis remarked more than two decades ago, "both the teaching and studying of Shakespeare are exacting, often frustrating tasks, necessitating thorough, perceptive, informed study, for which there are no painless shortcuts or easy formulas" (1964, 240).

Previous Research

Approaches

Researchers have left us more information about the methods we should use in teaching Shake-

speare's language than about the troublesome characteristics on which we ought to focus. First, even though they have not discussed the teaching of Shakespeare's language in particular, those concerned with schema theory have provided valuable information about general pedagogical principles. They have indicated that all of us accommodate new information by relating it to information we already possess; that knowledge does not consist of strings of independent details but rather of structured collections in which details have relationships; and that we sometimes require not only new information about subject matter (content schemata) but also new knowledge that will help us understand structures used to organize discourse (textual schemata) (Mayer 1984; Barnett 1984; Carr and Wixson 1985/86; Nagy 1988, in press; Marzano et al. 1988). Thus, proponents of schema theory have indicated that we must help our students move toward the strange by taking them through the familiar; that we must help students find value in new facts by enabling them to form connections between those new facts and others; and that we must sometimes introduce to them ways of manipulating language that they are neither prepared to perceive nor inclined to accept. I will make clear the importance of these points as I describe the general strategies I have followed in the practice section of this booklet.

As schema theory has been providing information about learning in general, many teachers at several levels have been providing one major recommendation about the teaching of Shakespeare's language in particular. Performances, rehearsal activities, readings, and assorted dramatic exercises, these teachers tell us, can help students associate themselves with the speakers of Shakespeare's lines and, thus, help students associate Shakespeare's language with their own (see especially Carter 1983; Swander 1984; Frey 1984; Gilbert 1984; O'Brien 1984).

Difficulties Caused by Shakespeare's Language

Whereas those concerned with pedagogical methods have left us useful advice in recent years, observers concerned with the specific difficulties caused by Shakespeare's language have left us only one strong recommendation: to give some special attention to the most troublesome kinds of words, familiar words (such as "still," "abuse," "gentle," and "discover") used with unexpected meanings. For example, F. P. Wilson (1941, 172–74) devotes a considerable part of a very famous essay to such words, and Alfred Harbage (1963, 14–17), several pages of an even more famous book. Stuart Omans recommends that students be asked to develop lists of troublesome words—including familiar words that have changed in meaning—so that they will not have to continually "rediscover the wheel—underwater . . ." (1973, 14). In addition, George Price provides a list of deceptive words as well as the following warning: "Editors occasionally gloss these words in their notes to the plays; but precisely because the words recur so often, they cannot be noted regularly" (1962, 13).

Less common are observers who tell us to give special attention to the difficulties caused by strange arrangements of words. Among the few who mention such arrangements are R. C. Bennett, George Kernodle, and Laura Hapke. Bennett (1968/69, 57) reports on the problems such strange arrangements cause for foreign students. Kernodle—noting that subordinate elements in Shakespeare's sentences often separate related parts—advises: "It is good practice to read separately the subject, verb, and object, to make sure the basic structure of the sentence is understood before adding the subordinate elements" (1949, 40). And Hapke (1984), whose observations are similar to Kernodle's, also writes on the value of working with students to identify the subjects and verbs of difficult Shakespearean sentences.

Even more rare are comments on the problems caused for readers by Shakespeare's omissions of syllables, parts of syllables, and words. Ordinarily, writers mention such omissions only in passing, if at all. Kernodle, for instance, merely says that "Shakespeare is often very compact and elliptical . . ." (1949, 39), and Harbage merely provides a few illustrations to support his assertion that one finds in Shakespeare "ellipsis of every possible kind" (1963, 20).

In sum, although for many years scholars have been providing valuable information on the characteristics of Shakespeare's language (see particularly Abbott 1870; Franz 1924; Hulme 1962 and 1972; Barber 1976; Brook 1976; Hussey 1982; and

Blake 1983), observers have shown little concern for the main difficulties presented by that language to student readers. Only in 1986, 1987, and 1988, in fact, in seminars and workshops provided by the Shakespeare Association of America, NCTE, and the Folger Shakespeare Library, have signs appeared of a significant general interest in such difficulties.

Additional Research

Activities

During the past four years, I have taught Shakespeare to graduate students in English, to undergraduates from various majors, and to twenty high school sophomores in two workshops supported by the National Council of Teachers of English. In working with these students, I have made special efforts to identify their principal weaknesses and needs as readers.

In 1985 and 1986, I gave lengthy diagnostic quizzes to thirty undergraduates and to all twenty of the high school students. I also met with each of the high school students and with twenty-eight undergraduates in diagnostic paraphrase sessions. In each of these sessions, I gave the student a cutting of about fifty lines from one of Shakespeare's plays, and, after a short introduction, asked the student to mark every word, phrase, clause, or sentence with which he or she wanted help. Then, as I provided questions and bits of information, the student worked to produce a word-for-word paraphrase of the entire selection. Through these quizzes and paraphrase sessions, I was trying to answer two main questions. First, what characteristics of Shakespeare's language most confuse students? Second, are students, in general, able to identify most of the elements that trouble them when reading Shakespeare?

Furthermore, in 1985 I composed a set of course notes on Shakespeare's language. In these notes I included information and illustrations of the expected kind, but I also included descriptions of writing assignments that I thought students could use to become more comfortable with the language of Shakespeare's plays. I used these notes in my graduate and undergraduate classes and also in the two high school workshops.

Since 1984 I have also worked with acting groups at every level, and I have frequently asked students to imitate Shakespeare's practices in their own compositions. In addition, I have sometimes given quizzes on the course notes, and I have occasionally asked students to analyze grammatically sentences from Shakespeare's plays. I have also asked advanced students to write elaborate essays on the speaking styles presented by various Shakespearean characters.

The Most Troublesome Practices of Shakespeare's Speakers

First, my investigations strongly support the most common assertion made by earlier observers. When students encounter familiar words used with unexpected meanings, they are indeed likely to misread and misunderstand the speakers' meanings. In fact, when I asked students to look for elements with which they needed assistance in Shakespearean passages, they very rarely mentioned such words at all; they looked chiefly for strange words instead—words such as "countenance," "prithee," "pranked," and "swain"— thinking that most of their difficulties as readers were caused by these unfamiliar words. Also, most students had great difficulty surrendering the familiar meanings of familiar words, even when those meanings were absurdly inappropriate for the contexts in which Shakespeare's characters were using the words.

Second, my investigations show that strange arrangements of words in the speeches of Shakespeare's characters are much more likely to produce severe impediments for students than observers have supposed. Only very rarely do students recognize that the unusual arrangements of words in Shakespearean sentences may be impeding them as readers. Further, most students are not prepared to solve the problems that such arrangements cause even after they become aware that these arrangements exist. Many students simply do not have the training to identify the major elements of a clause and to put those elements into a more commonplace, understandable order. Others, although well schooled in grammatical analysis, have never learned to use their analytical skills as readers.

Third, my investigations show that Shakespeare's omissions also cause difficulties that are much more severe than observers have commonly supposed. Omissions of syllables and parts of syllables frequently distract and slow students. In addition, clauses with missing words often confuse or baffle them. Although, as speakers of English, all students have learned to add words mentally to the speeches of others in order to understand them, most students do not know consciously that they have that skill; they do not perceive that they must use it as readers; and they do not easily use it, even under pressure, with the works of Shakespeare.

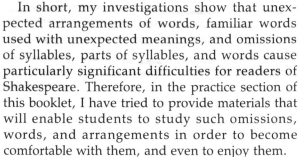

In short, my investigations show that unexpected arrangements of words, familiar words used with unexpected meanings, and omissions of syllables, parts of syllables, and words cause particularly significant difficulties for readers of Shakespeare. Therefore, in the practice section of this booklet, I have tried to provide materials that will enable students to study such omissions, words, and arrangements in order to become comfortable with them, and even to enjoy them.

Teachers should not think, however, that students' reactions to omissions, unexpected arrangements, and deceptive words are the only ones that demand careful attention. Indeed, other reactions, which I have not mentioned in the practice section, also require concern, and I can best introduce these by stating some assumptions that I have developed during the past four years:

1. Most students will understand incompletely the common and very significant pronouns, "thou," "thee," "thy," "thine," and "thyself."

2. Most students will be slow to notice the emphases produced when Shakespeare's characters repeat words, the roots or stems of words, sounds, rhythms, or constructions; consequently, most students will often fail to give proper weight to certain words and will fail to interpret sentences accurately.

3. Most students will have difficulty perceiving the associations that occur when speakers use metaphor and personification and will therefore have difficulty using such associations to build up ideas about the speakers' chief concerns.

4. Most students will have difficulty understanding wordplay, especially when the

wordplay is bawdy and expresses a speaker's resistance to intimate, tender relationships.

5. Most students will refuse to assign unexpected meanings to familiar affixes, even when such meanings are clearly intended by the playwright's speakers.

6. Most students will often be confused by pronouns that have no specific antecedents and by pronouns that have no antecedents nearby.

7. Most students will become distracted or perplexed when Shakespearean characters use infinitives where we would not; when they introduce objects or reflexive pronouns where we would not; or when they employ auxiliary verbs different from the ones that we would choose.

The evidence that I have collected also indicates that these assumptions might well be legitimate conclusions. Certainly, they have served me well in my work with both high school students and undergraduates.

Practice

As I have indicated, the practice section itself contains three sections. The first of these three sections treats unexpected arrangements of words; the second deals with omissions of syllables, parts of syllables, and words; and the third concerns familiar words that appear either sometimes or always with unexpected meanings in Shakespeare's plays.

Sections 1 and 2 are quite similar. Each section presents a series of worksheets for students and an introduction to those worksheets for teachers. In preparing these worksheets, I have kept in mind two of the points elaborated in schema theory: first, that we must sometimes develop new knowledge about the conventions of organized discourse in order to understand unfamiliar texts, and second, that we always accommodate new knowledge by relating it to old or existing knowledge. Thus, to help the students develop new knowledge about conventions, I have described the syntactical schemes that underlie some of Shakespeare's unexpected arrangements of words as well as some of his troublesome omissions.

Further, to help the students relate the new knowledge to existing knowledge, I have shown how these syntactical schemes differ from or resemble schemes that the students themselves use in modern English. I have also shown the students how to transform Shakespeare's unfamiliar schemes into familiar ones by rearranging words or by adding words. In addition, I have asked the students to follow my examples and make similar transformations themselves. I have also urged the students to produce unusual schemes while writing original pieces in familiar, modern English.

Section 3 differs strikingly from sections 1 and 2. It does not present worksheets. It presents, chiefly, a collection of familiar words and some information about the unexpected meanings those words can carry. In developing this section, however, as in developing sections 1 and 2, I have kept in mind some major points included in schema theory. Thus, I have organized the words into groups, and I have shown each of the words at work in at least one sentence, or a piece of a sentence, from one of Shakespeare's plays (for information on the benefits students receive from seeing words in groups and in syntactical contexts, see Carr and Wixson 1985/86; Stahl 1985/86; and Nagy 1988, in press).

In my introduction to section 3, I have presented some assignments that teachers can use in conjunction with the vocabulary materials. The assignments ask students to create new groupings for some of the words and to use words with their unfamiliar meanings in original compositions. As writers on vocabulary instruction emphasize, such assignments can help students both understand and remember new information about words (Carr and Wixson 1985/86; Stahl 1985/86).

In preparing sections 1, 2, and 3 of this booklet, I have used passages from many different plays. My favorite sources have been *Hamlet*, *Othello*, and *King Lear*, but I have also included several passages from each of the following works: *Richard III, The Taming of the Shrew, Romeo and Juliet, A Midsummer Night's Dream, Richard II, 1 Henry IV, Julius Caesar, Twelfth Night, As You Like It, All's Well That Ends Well, Macbeth, Antony and Cleopatra, The Winter's Tale,* and *The Tempest.* Since all are plays that teachers frequently assign and acting companies often perform, most students will probably find some acquaintance with them useful. My texts for the plays come from the Pelican collection: *William Shakespeare: The Complete Works* (Harbage 1969). Because long-accepted principles for the editing of Shakespeare's plays are now being challenged by numerous scholars, generally respected editions of the plays are hard to find. However, the Pelican texts, which are easily obtainable in paperback editions, have won greater acceptance in recent decades than most competing versions, and they are often used in the schools. Readers should understand that the numbers assigned to lines in other texts (particularly in scenes that include prose) and also the line readings in other texts will differ sometimes from those presented by the Pelican text.

[handwritten: Pelican]

The Context for Studying Shakespeare's Language

High school and college students alike are eager to find their places in society—to know where, exactly, they fit in—and they want to interact dramatically with one another, to express and clarify their own motives, to learn about the motives of others, and to analyze the major problems that commonly arise in human relationships. Through a number of activities, students can make the study of Shakespeare's language a means, a pro-

[handwritten: Activities]

logue, or an accompaniment to their pursuit of immediate social goals.

First, students can communicate with one another by sharing the original compositions that they produce in their study of Shakespeare's language. Second, after discussing the language of Shakespearean scenes in small groups, students can discuss the motives of the characters who appear in those scenes, and they can compare those characters with real people who are important to their everyday lives. Third, as students study Shakespeare's language in the relatively restrained ways urged by this booklet, they can also participate in the more physical and more emotional explorations of language made possible by rehearsal exercises and theatrical games. Finally, after working with materials from this booklet, students can use their knowledge of Shakespeare's language in performances of scenes from Shakespeare's plays. Through such performances, they can express themselves and relate to one another intensely in the safe, pretending space of the stage.

In short, through various activities that are suitable for the classroom, students can draw Shakespeare's language out of the past and give to it the flesh, fabric, rhythms, and breath of present reality. They can place this language within the contexts of their own lives and use it to make discoveries about themselves.

2 PRACTICE

SECTION 1: SHAKESPEARE'S UNUSUAL ARRANGEMENTS OF WORDS—EIGHT WORKSHEETS FOR THE CLASSROOM

Introduction

When you and I and our students read an English sentence, we expect the positions of the words to guide us toward understanding. First, from each word's position, we expect to receive information about the word's *role* in the sentence. Second, because we assume that a word is most closely tied to the words that are near it, we expect a word's position to tell us much about its *relationships* with other words.

But sometimes writers do the unexpected. Sometimes writers give words with certain roles positions that words with such roles do not usually occupy in English. And sometimes, too, writers separate words that are closely related. Consequently, the texts that we use in our schools sometimes present words in positions that our students find misleading, and in their efforts to read such texts, many students become perplexed. Further, not being aware that they have wanted guidance from positions of the words and been denied it, many students cannot know the causes of their confusion, and they must simply remain confused. Thus, they proceed as readers while comprehending only parts of many sentences, only parts of many pages, and only parts of numerous texts; and even though they may try to console themselves by saying, "Well, we just have to read for the general sense of passages anyway," at some level they know that, reading in bits and pieces, they are missing the general sense more often than they are finding it, and at that same level, they experience the infuriating emptiness of failure.

Such painful descents into fragmentary reading occur with particular frequency when students are working with Shakespeare, as the information provided in the preceding theory and research section reveals. The characters of Shakespeare's plays often arrange words in unexpected ways, and, consequently, students often find the English of those works to be distant from the English that they have learned to understand.

Still, we can do much to make Shakespeare's difficult arrangements of words less taxing in the classroom. The comments and performances of my own students lead me to offer five recommendations:

1. Choose several sets of words, and arrange each set in two, three, four, or five ways to form differing sentences. Through these sentences, reveal to your students that they do indeed look to the positions of words for cues about the words' roles and relationships. In addition, through these sentences, present unexpected arrangements similar to those that occur most often in Shakespeare's plays.

2. Quote from Shakespeare's plays passages that present unexpected arrangements of words, and, to help the students link Shakespeare's language with their own, associate these Shakespearean arrangements with unusual arrangements that you formed in your own contemporary English sentences. In addition, give the words in the Shakespearean passages more familiar, more understandable, arrangements.

3. After you have rearranged the words of some Shakespearean passages, quote additional passages and ask the students to rearrange the words of those.

4. Have the students read *aloud* all of the revised pieces that you and they have formed. Have them also read *aloud* all of the original Shakespearean passages. Urge them to find connections among words as they read the

revised pieces, and urge them to emphasize these same connections as they read the original Shakespearean passages.

5. **Have your students form clauses that contain unexpected arrangements of words similar to some that appear in Shakespeare's plays.** Have the students do so, sometimes, for reasons that are similar to Shakespeare's.

More useful than these bare recommendations, however, will be the eight worksheets presented in this section. These worksheets provide sentences, quotations, revisions, and instructions of the kind I have just mentioned, and they provide them in a carefully structured sequence. The few paragraphs that follow will introduce these worksheets.

Remarks on the Eight Worksheets

Worksheet 1

In the first worksheet, I have presented different versions of sentences written in contemporary English, for the two reasons that I mentioned in the first of my recommendations. First, I have done so to help students become aware of the meanings that they expect the positions of words to have. In effect, even though I have shunned the terms of traditional grammar, I have tried to show the students that they commonly operate with the following assumptions:

● In a declarative clause, the first of the major elements will be the subject, the second will be the predicate, and the third (if there is a third) will be the object or some other complement.

● In a declarative clause, at least one of the major elements—a subject, predicate, or complement—will appear near the beginning.

● Related words will appear close to one another.

In addition, I have presented the model sentences that appear in worksheet 1 in order to introduce the major types of odd arrangements that occur in Shakespeare's plays. Through these sentences, I have provided several clauses in which predicates or complements come first—rather than second or third—among the major elements.

I have also provided a long clause in which related parts are separated. And I have provided another clause in which no major parts appear near the clause's beginning.

As I have already indicated, however, the worksheet itself does not include such terms as "subject," "predicate," "object," and "complement." In fact, the only terms from traditional grammar that I have used in any of the eight worksheets are "sentence," "clause," and "syllable." The traditional terms can frustrate students who are unfamiliar with them. They can also lead students who have been trained in their use to concentrate on gaining new knowledge about English constructions, not on developing additional strategies as readers—and above all, these worksheets should provoke concern with strategies for understanding sophisticated texts.

The material in worksheet 1 may be combined with material included in worksheets 6, 7, and 8. These four worksheets—unlike worksheets 2, 3, 4, and 5—do not press students to discover the meanings of sentences through analytical thinking. Rather, they invite students to explore both the English language and their attitudes toward it playfully. I have often used parts of these four worksheets together in the classroom to prepare students for the activities required in worksheets 2 through 5.

Worksheets 2, 3, 4, and 5

In the second, third, fourth, and fifth worksheets, I have presented difficult Shakespearean passages and asked the students to rearrange the words. However, before asking the students to analyze and alter any passage, I have analyzed and changed a similar passage myself. I have thus provided examples for the students to follow, not analytical rules for them to obey.

Furthermore, near the start of each worksheet, I have repeated at least one unusual modern clause from worksheet 1. I intend for these clauses to serve as intermediate formations. Commonplace in diction and content, but exceptional in syntactical patterns, they should help students proceed from their own conversational English to the often unexpected English of Shakespeare's plays.

I have also tried to assist the students by emphasizing very strongly two directions about revising. Over and over, I have insisted that the students should give to Shakespeare's words arrangements that are similar to those they would really use in conversations with friends. I have also insisted, over and over, that they should not add words as they are rearranging, should not omit words, and should not change any words for others. Such repetitions help some students (but certainly not all) resist two temptations that commonly arise: (1) the temptation to change a passage only slightly, not making the difficult transformations necessary to form a truly conversational pattern, and (2) the temptation to produce, not a disciplined rearrangement of words, but an ill-considered, hastily-wrought paraphrase or summary.

In addition, I have insisted in these worksheets that the students should read *aloud* all of the new and all of the original arrangements of Shakespeare's words. Students can discover connections among the words of each piece more easily by reading them aloud than by reading them silently. Then, as they read the original lines aloud, students can remain sensitive to the relationships they have discovered and can make these relationships evident to others. Furthermore, by reading aloud, students can discover that Shakespeare's language is, above all else, a vehicle for human emotions and is therefore a medium through which they can express themselves.

In concluding my remarks on these four worksheets, I would make explicit what their various lengths imply. Worksheets 2 and 5, which are considerably longer than worksheets 3 and 4, deal with arrangements of words that are not only troublesome, but also especially common in Shakespeare's plays.

The Final Worksheets

Worksheets 6, 7, and 8 ask students to imitate some of Shakespeare's practices by forming clever, unexpected, and artistic arrangements of words. Indirectly, these worksheets also encourage students to experience some of the pleasures that Shakespeare experienced in forming such arrangements—including the pleasures of making rhythms and rhymes.

Worksheets 6 and 7 simply ask students to create clauses similar to those that preceding worksheets asked them to understand. In effect, they emphasize types of clauses: clauses in which major elements are oddly ordered and clauses in which related words are separated.

Worksheet 8, however, emphasizes motives that provoked Shakespeare to arrange words in unexpected ways, and it asks students to let such motives provoke them, too, during a few exercises. The motives in question, as the worksheet itself suggests, are chiefly artistic. When he separated related words, when he put complements before subjects and predicates, and, usually, when he put predicates before subjects, Shakespeare was not following the basic, conversational patterns of his own day—for the elementary, conversational patterns of English were, in Shakespeare's day, almost the same as they are now. Rather, Shakespeare was departing from the elementary speech patterns of his day for poetic or dramatic purposes. Sometimes, for instance, he arranged words in unexpected ways because he wanted characters to express themselves through elaborate rhetorical figures or through nonsensical combinations. Most often, however, he formed unexpected arrangements because (1) he wanted to put rhyming words at the ends of lines and (2) he wanted to put stressed syllables in locations where his interests as a poet—a maker of rhythms—demanded that he put them. Because these last two motives are the most significant ones for Shakespeare, they are the ones I have explained in worksheet 8 and the ones I have asked the students to assume.

Finally, I should add a comment on evaluation that is pertinent to all eight of the worksheets, and especially to the last three. Simply, in preparing these worksheets, I never intended to produce items that would test for knowledge and make possible the accurate grading of students. Rather, I was hoping to develop handouts that would help students perceive and change their habits as readers; that would help them discuss language with one another; that would enable them to experience verbal variations from the inside looking out, as artists, having fun and playing games; that would generate materials for classroom performances; and, finally, that would yield occasions for good-natured laughter. Thus, I think on any of the worksheets a grade more sophisticated than a simple "pass" or "fail" might be very difficult to assign.

WORKSHEET 1: INTRODUCTION TO UNUSUAL ARRANGEMENTS OF WORDS

Part A

The six sentences that follow are all very much alike. The same four words—and only those four—appear in each of the six sentences. Furthermore, each of the six sentences delivers the very same message that each of the other five delivers. Still, no one sentence in the group is exactly the same as any other—each sentence has its own, special, unique arrangement of words. After you have read and compared the six sentences, answer the questions that follow them.

1. Ate the sandwich I.
2. I the sandwich ate.
3. I ate the sandwich.
4. Ate I the sandwich.
5. The sandwich I ate.
6. The sandwich ate I.

Question: Which of these six sentences would you use if you wanted someone else to understand your meaning quickly and easily? *Answer:* Sentence number _____.

Question: Which of these sentences would you be most likely to create while speaking in a relaxed way with a friend? *Answer:* Sentence number _____.

Question: In how many different positions does the word "sandwich" appear in these six sentences? *Answer:* In _____ positions.

Question: In how many different positions does the word "ate" appear in these six sentences? *Answer:* In _____ positions.

Question: In how many different positions does the word "I" appear in these six sentences? *Answer:* In _____ positions.

Question: How does the clearest sentence of the six differ from all of the other sentences? (If you cannot answer this question now, leave the following lines blank and wait for the class discussion.) *Answer:* _____

_____

Question: Which of the six sentences is most like "Peculiar was the thief"? *Answer:* Sentence number _____.

Question: Which of the six sentences is most like "The thief was peculiar"? *Answer:* Sentence number _____.

Part B

The two sentences that follow are also much alike. Sentence one delivers the same message that sentence two delivers, and sentence one contains the very same words that sentence two contains. But the arrangement of words in one sentence is quite different from the arrangement of words in the other. After you have read and compared the sentences, answer the questions that follow them.

1. Ralph saw Martha on the channel 9 late show at twelve o'clock, while eating pistachio ice cream, before turning to homework.
2. On the channel 9 late show at twelve o'clock, while eating pistachio ice cream, before turning to homework, Ralph saw Martha.

Question: Which of the two sentences would you use if you wanted someone to understand your meaning quickly and easily? *Answer:* Sentence number _____.

Question: What are the three major elements in each sentence?

Answer: _____, _____, and _____.

Question: Where do the three major elements appear in sentence two?

Answer: _____.

Part C

Following are two more sentences that are very much alike. The same words that occur in one sentence also occur in the other, and the meaning that one delivers, the other delivers as well. But, as the two sentences in part B differ in their arrangements of words, so do the two sentences that follow. First, read and compare the sentences, and then answer the questions that come after them.

1. While my cousin Joan was walking sadly home from school, she heard, far away in the afternoon, little children happily singing.
2. While home from school sadly was my cousin Joan walking, little children far away happily singing in the afternoon she heard.

Question: Which of these two sentences would you use if you wanted someone else to understand your meaning quickly and easily?

Answer: Sentence number _____.

Question: In sentence two, several words that are closely related to "walking" appear at some distance from "walking." What are two of those words?

Answer: _____ and _____.

Question: If you were asked to make sentence two clearer, what word or words would you first move closer to "heard"?

Answer: _____.

Fun and Games

Give an unusual arrangement to the words in each of these sentences:

1. Joan went to school.

_____

2. Martha quickly called Ralph on the telephone.

_____

3. Mary laughed and sang when she saw that her present for her sixth birthday, which came on the Tuesday before Thanksgiving, was a new bicycle with a red seat, chrome fenders, and yellow tires.

_____

_____

_____

WORKSHEET 2: UNUSUAL
SEQUENCES OF WORDS I

Introduction

As you were reading worksheet 1, you found:

> Peculiar was the thief,

and

> The sandwich I ate.

These two sentences present similar, and rather strange, constructions. First, each of the sentences contains three major elements: in "Peculiar was the thief" the three are "Peculiar," "was," and "thief"; in "The sandwich I ate," the three are "sandwich," "I," and "ate." Second, each sentence presents, as the first of its three major elements, the element that you and I would ordinarily put third. Usually we would not say, "*Peculiar* was the thief." Rather, we would say, "The thief was *peculiar*." And usually we would not say, "The *sandwich* I ate." Instead, we would say, "I ate the *sandwich*."

In Shakespeare's plays you will often find sequences of words just as unusual as those in "Peculiar was the thief" and "The sandwich I ate." And when you find such odd sequences in Shakespeare's plays, you will frequently discover them in sentences that contain words with unknown or unexpected meanings and sometimes in sentences of considerable length. Consequently, you may often be very confused by the sentences to which they contribute.

To help you prepare for such unexpected sequences in Shakespeare, I have provided eight passages from the plays. In each of these, a character puts first, among three major elements of a clause, the element that you and I would ordinarily put third.

To introduce each of these passages I have said a few words about the speaker. In addition, I have reacted to each of the first two passages as I have asked you to react to each of the other six: (1) I have identified the major elements of the troublesome clause in each passage, and (2) I have put the words of the entire passage in the order I would use if I were talking casually with a friend. These first two passages I have labeled "My Passages" and the other six I have labeled "Your Passages."

I have put bullets in the left margin to identify sections where you should make responses in writing. Whenever you come to a section that asks you to rearrange words, always follow these two cardinal rules:

> As you rearrange, give the words the order you would probably give them in conversation with a friend.

> As you rearrange, do not omit any word, add any word, or change any word for another word.

My Passages

My Passage One

The following lines come from one of Iago's soliloquies in *Othello.* Often within his soliloquies, Iago provides details about his schemes to undo Othello, Desdemona, and Cassio, and in this one he says:

> Three lads of Cyprus—noble swelling spirits,
> That hold their honors in a wary distance,
> The very elements of this warlike isle—
> Have I to-night flustered with flowing cups.
> And they watch too.
>
> (2.3.51–55)

The troublesome clause here begins in the first line (with "Three lads") and ends at the fourth (with "flowing cups"). The major elements are "lads," "Have . . . flustered," and "I." In ordinary conversation, I would put "I" first, "have flustered" second, and "lads" third. My sequence would therefore be: "I have flustered lads." But Iago puts "lads" first, "have" second, and "I" third, and then he brings in "flustered" (which he has separated from "have"). Thus, his sequence is: "Lads have I flustered."

Iago's lines become clearer when I put his words in an order I would use in conversation:

> To-night *I have flustered* with flowing cups three *lads* of Cyprus—noble swelling spirits, the very elements of this warlike isle, that hold their honors in a wary distance—and they watch, too.

My Passage Two

In the following passage from *King Lear,* Albany is talking to his wife, Goneril. He is attacking her and her sister, Regan, for the hostility they have shown the King, their father:

> A father, and a gracious agèd man,
> Whose reverence even the head-lugged bear would lick,
> Most barbarous, most degenerate, have you madded.
> (4.2.41–43)

The troublesome clause here includes, "A father, and a gracious agèd man . . . / Most barbarous, most degenerate, have you madded." The major elements in this clause are "you," "have . . . madded," and "father, and . . . man." In ordinary conversation, I would put "you" first, "have madded" second, and "father and man" third. My sequence would therefore be: "You have madded a father and a man." But Albany puts "father and man" first, puts "have" second, puts "you" third, and then brings in "madded" (which he has separated from "have"). Consequently, his sequence is: "A father and a man have you madded."

Albany's statement becomes clearer when I put his major elements in a more ordinary order:

> You—most barbarous, most degenerate—*have madded* a *father,* and a gracious agèd *man,* whose reverence even the head-lugged bear would lick.

Your Passages

Your Passage One

In the following passage from *Othello,* Othello is stressing to his wife, Desdemona, the importance of a gift that she has lost:

> That handkerchief
> Did an Egyptian to my mother give.
> (3.4.55–56)

Activities

- List the three major elements in Othello's sentence.

  _____, _____, and _____

- Rearrange Othello's words. Give them the order you would probably give them in ordinary conversation.

  _____

  _____

  _____

Your Passage Two

In *Romeo and Juliet,* the Prince begins the final speech of the play by saying:

> A glooming peace this morning with it brings.
> (5.3.305)

Activities

- List the three major elements in the Prince's clause.

  _____, _____, and _____

- Rearrange the Prince's words. Give them the order you would probably give them in ordinary conversation.

  _____

Your Passage Three

In *Hamlet,* after Hamlet promises to take revenge on his father's killer, the Ghost of his father responds:

> I fine thee apt,
> And duller shouldst thou be than the fat weed
> That roots itself in ease on Lethe wharf,
> Wouldst thou not stir in this.
> (1.5.31–34)

Activities

- List the three major elements in "duller shouldst thou be than the fat weed."

  _____, _____, and _____

- Rearrange the words of the Ghost's entire sentence (all four lines). Give the words the order you would probably give them in ordinary conversation.

_____

_____

_____

Your Passage Four

In *The Tempest*, the magician, Prospero, tells his servant spirit, Ariel:

> Thy shape invisible retain thou still.
> (4.1.185)

Activities

- List the three major elements in Prospero's clause.

  _____, _____, and _____

- Rearrange Prospero's words. Give them the order you would probably give them in ordinary conversation.

_____

Your Passage Five

Perdita, in *The Winter's Tale*, believes herself to be a mere shepherdess, and she is slightly embarrassed that Florizel, the Prince of Bohemia, has dressed himself as a country fellow (a "swain") to be near her. Thus, she gently chides Florizel:

> Your high self,
> The gracious mark o' th' land, you have obscured
> With a swain's wearing. . . .
> (4.4.7–9)

Activities

- List the three major elements in Perdita's clause.

  _____, _____, and _____

- Rearrange Perdita's words. Give them the order you would probably give them in ordinary conversation.

_____

_____

_____

Your Passage Six

In the opening scene of *The First Part of Henry IV*, King Henry complains about the behavior of young Henry Percy, commonly known as Hotspur:

> The prisoners
> Which he in this adventure hath surprised
> To his own use he keeps, and sends me word
> I shall have none but Mordake Earl of Fife.
> (1.1.92–95)

Activities

- List the three major elements in ''The prisoners / . . . To his own use he keeps. . . .''
  _____, _____, and _____

- Rearrange the words of the King's sentence (all four lines). Give them the order you would probably give them in ordinary conversation.

_____

_____

_____

Reading Aloud

After you have rearranged your six passages, go back to the first passage that I rearranged. Read my new version of passage one aloud two or three times. As you read, emphasize the same words that you would emphasize if you were speaking the lines in everyday conversation. Next, read the original Shakespearean passage aloud two or three times, and be careful to produce, again, the same emphases you created in your reading of the revised passage. Then follow the same procedure with the original and revised versions of the other seven passages (my second passage and your six passages).

Such readings—if you do read *aloud*—will make you more sensitive to the roles and relationships of Shakespeare's actual words, and they will help you change yourself from a merely ordinary reader to one who truly comprehends Shakespeare—word by word and line by line. They will also prepare you to interpret Shakespeare's plays and to express yourself through them as a performer.

WORKSHEET 3: UNUSUAL
SEQUENCES OF WORDS II

Introduction

In worksheet 2 you considered some Shakespearean clauses that resemble "Peculiar was the thief" and "The sandwich I ate." In this worksheet, you will consider some Shakespearean clauses that resemble "Ate I the sandwich" and "Ate the sandwich I." In each of these, the element that we would expect to come second among the major elements comes first instead. Usually we would not say either "*Ate* the sandwich I" or "*Ate* I the sandwich." Rather, we would say, "I *ate* the sandwich."

To help you adjust to Shakespearean constructions similar to "Ate I the sandwich" and "Ate the sandwich I," I have quoted the following four passages from the plays. In each of these, a character puts first among the major elements of a clause the element that we would usually put second.

To introduce the four passages, I have said a bit about the speaker of each one. I have also reacted to the first two passages as I have asked you to react to the other two. I have listed the major elements in the troublesome clause of each passage, and I have given the words of each passage the order I would give them in conversation with a friend.

I have again put bullets in the margins to mark sections where you should respond in writing. I have also retained the labels "My Passages" and "Your Passages."

Whenever you come to a section in this worksheet that asks you to rearrange, follow the two cardinal rules:

As you rearrange, give the words the order you would probably give them in conversation with a friend.

As you rearrange, do not omit any word, add any word, or change any word for another word.

My Passages

My Passage One

In the opening scene of *Romeo and Juliet,* Montague says of the melancholy Romeo:

> Away from light steals home my heavy son
> And private in his chamber pens himself. . . .
> (1.1.135–36)

In the first of these lines, Montague presents "son" and "steals"—the two main elements of his clause—in an unexpected order. He puts first the element that we would ordinarily put second. Most of us would not usually say, "Away from light *steals* home my heavy *son*." Instead, we would say:

> My heavy *son steals* home away from light.

My Passage Two

In the bloodstained world of *Richard III*, one of the most bitter characters is old Queen Margaret. When she speaks the following lines, she has just been expressing delight in the misfortunes of her enemies, whose prosperity has begun "to mellow / And drop into the rotten mouth of death" (4.4.1–2):

> A dire induction am I witness to,
> And will to France, hoping the consequence
> Will prove as bitter, black, and tragical.
>   (4.4.5–7)

The clause that Margaret creates in this first line contains three main elements: "am, " "I," and "witness." These she introduces in an uncommon order. Although we would expect "am" to be the second of the major elements, she makes it the first. The sequence is therefore, "Am I witness." A more ordinary sequence would be, "I am witness," and a more ordinary arrangement for the entire clause would be:

> I am witness to a dire induction.

Your Passages

Your Passage One

In the following lines from *Measure for Measure,* Lucio explains to Isabella that the Duke's office is temporarily filled by a deputy, Angelo (the "his place" of Lucio's first line means "the Duke's place"):

> Upon his place,
> And with full line of his authority,
> Governs Lord Angelo, a man whose blood
> Is very snow-broth. . . .
>   (1.4.55–58)

Activities

- List the two major elements in "Upon his place, / And with full line of his authority, / Governs Lord Angelo. . . ."

  _____ and _____

- Rearrange the words of Lucio's entire statement (all four lines).

  _____

  _____

  _____

Your Passage Two

In the following lines from the final scene of *Hamlet*, Hamlet is describing his escape from Rosencrantz and Guildenstern:

> Up from my cabin,
> My sea-gown scarfed about me, in the dark
> Groped I to find out them. . . .
>
> (5.2.12–14)

Activities

- List the two major elements in Hamlet's clause.

  _____ and _____

- Rearrange Hamlet's words.

  _____

  _____

Reading Aloud

After you rearrange your two passages, return to the first of my passages. Read aloud the version of the passage I created by rearranging its words. Then read aloud the original Shakespearean passage. Follow the same procedure for each of the three remaining passages (my one passage and your two passages). The new version of each passage should help you become sensitive to the roles and relationships of each character's actual words.

WORKSHEET 4: CONSTRUCTIONS
THAT DELAY

Introduction

In worksheet 2 you considered Shakespearean clauses that resemble "The sandwich I ate" and "Peculiar was the thief." In worksheet 3, you considered Shakespearean clauses that resemble "Ate the sandwich I" and "Ate I the sandwich." In this fourth worksheet, you will consider some Shakespearean clauses that resemble:

> On the channel 9 late show at twelve o'clock, while eating pistachio ice cream,
> before turning to homework, Ralph saw Martha.

This—as you have probably remarked already—is a very peculiar clause indeed. In constructing it, I have not followed one of the main conventions we commonly accept as speakers of English. Usually, in forming a clause, we try to put at least one of its major elements near its beginning. This clause about Ralph and Martha, however, delays. It makes us wait to hear any one of its three major elements: "Ralph," "saw," and "Martha."

In Shakespeare's plays, clauses similar to this one—clauses that delay—appear frequently. In fact, you found two clauses of this type in worksheet 3. One appeared in the following lines, spoken by Lucio to Isabella:

> Upon his place,
> And with full line of his authority,
> Governs Lord Angelo, a man whose blood
> Is very snow-broth. . . .

The other appeared in Hamlet's lines to Horatio:

> Up from my cabin,
> My sea-gown scarfed about me, in the dark
> Groped I to find out them. . . .

In the first of these, the major elements are "Governs" and "Lord Angelo," and in the second, the major elements are "Groped" and "I." In each passage, no major element appears until the third line of the statement. Thus, each of the clauses delays.

In the following four passages, you will find four more clauses that delay. I have briefly introduced the speaker of each of these passages. I have also reacted to the first passage as I have asked you to react to each of the other three: (1) I have listed the major elements in the troublesome clause of that passage, and (2) I have given the words of the passage the order I would probably give them in conversation with a friend.

I have put bullets in the margins to identify sections where your written responses are required. In this worksheet, as in worksheets 2 and 3, always follow the two cardinal rules:

> As you rearrange, give the words the order you would probably give them in conversation with a friend.

> As you rearrange, do not omit any word, add any word, or change any word for another word.

My Passage

In the following lines from *Macbeth*, Macbeth tells the two murderers that not only Banquo, but also Banquo's young son, Fleance, must die (Macbeth's "with him," in the first line, means "with Banquo"):

> and with him,
> To leave no rubs nor botches in the work,
> Fleance his son, that keeps him company,
> Whose absence is no less material to me
> Than is his father's, must embrace the fate,
> Of that dark hour.
>
> (3.1.133–38)

The major elements of Macbeth's main clause are "Fleance," "must embrace," and "fate," and although Macbeth's statement is confusing for several reasons, it is difficult mainly because Macbeth does not put any of these major elements near the clause's beginning. Thus, the first operation necessary in making the passage clearer is the movement of "Fleance" to an earlier position. One rearrangement is the following:

> And *Fleance* his son (that keeps him company, whose absence is no less material to me than in his father's) *must embrace* the *fate* of that dark hour with him—to leave no rubs nor botches in the work.

Your Passages

Your Passage One

In the following lines from *King Lear*, Regan, one of Lear's daughters, is talking about her father and about the knights who ride with him (who form his "train"). In looking for a clause that delays, look at the second and third lines:

> He is attended with a desperate train,
> And what they may incense him to, being apt
> To have his ear abused, wisdom bids fear.
>
> (2.4.300–302)

Activities

● List the most important elements in: "what they may incense him to, being apt / To have his ear abused, wisdom bids fear" (note: "they" and "incense" are not among those most important elements).

_____,_____, and _____

● Rearrange the words of Regan's entire sentence (all three lines).

_____

_____

_____

Your Passage Two

In the following lines from *The Winter's Tale*, Perdita responds to Prince Florizel's description of her as a goddess:

> Sir, my gracious lord,
> To chide at your extremes it not becomes me—
> O, pardon, that I name them.
>
> (4.4.5–7)

Activities

- List the three major elements in "To chide at your extremes it not becomes me."

  _____, _____, and _____

- Rearrange the words of Perdita's entire statement (all three lines).

  _____

  _____

Your Passage Three

The speaker of the following passage is the Player King in "The Murder of Gonzago," a short play performed for the Danish court in *Hamlet*. The Player King is here beginning a speech in which he reminds his wife that they fell in love and married thirty years ago:

> Full thirty times hath Phoebus' cart gone round
> Neptune's salt wash and Tellus' orbèd ground. . . .
>
> (3.2.146–47)

Activities

- List the two major elements in the Player King's statement.

  _____ and _____

- Rearrange the Player King's words.

  _____

  _____

Reading Aloud

Before you leave worksheet 4, read aloud the passages you and I created by rearranging words, and also read aloud the original Shakespearean lines. Because such readings will help you associate unusual patterns with patterns that are more familiar, they will help you accept the strange patterns and enjoy them.

WORKSHEET 5: SEPARATIONS OF
RELATED PARTS

Introduction

Perhaps the strangest sentence that you considered in worksheet 1 was the second sentence on cousin Joan:

> While home from school sadly was my cousin Joan walking, little children far away happily singing in the afternoon she heard.

Several words that we would expect to see grouped with other words in this sentence appear at some distance from those other, related words. Thus, "was," "sadly," and "home from school" all appear at some distance from "walking"; "children" and "far away" both appear at some distance from "heard"; and "singing" appears at some distance from "children."

You can easily appreciate the confusing effects of such separations if you compare the version of the cousin Joan sentence that you just read with the following version. In this new version, the words that I separated in the preceding version are closer together. Consequently, the following version is much clearer:

> While my cousin Joan was walking sadly home from school, she heard, far away in the afternoon, little children happily singing.

As I have just made the cousin Joan sentence clearer by moving its related parts closer together, so you can make many sentences in Shakespeare's plays clearer by moving related parts in them nearer one another. The complications you will find in Shakespeare's work, however, are greater than I have indicated. In fact, in the speeches of his plays, you will find separations of five main kinds:

1. A character may separate the words of such a unit as "will go," "could have hit," "had known," "may think," "was eaten," or "has been seen."

2. A character may separate the words in such a unit as "I sang," "water will run," "house burned," "mail could arrive," "night may fall," or "council would decide."

3. A character may separate the parts of such a unit as "climbed the wall," "asked that I go," "believe it is a lie," "presents gold and silver," or "find the path."

4. A character may separate the parts of such a unit as "green trees," "man whose horse broke free," "days long and humid," "wonders that are present," or "you, walking in the sunlight."

5. A character may separate the parts of such a unit as "laughed loudly," "ran with great speed," "ate while singing," "went to town," "is accepted inside the house," or "were sent away."

In sections A through E, which follow, I have quoted passages that present separations of all five kinds. Each section contains two, three, or four passages.

I have briefly introduced the speaker of each passage. I have also reacted to the first passage in each section as I have asked you to react to every other passage in the section. First, I have listed, as a unit, closely related words that the speaker has separated. Second, by rearranging the words of the passage, I have put the separated words closer together.

I have put bullets in the margins to identify sections where you should provide written responses.

In this worksheet, as in worksheets 2, 3, and 4, always follow the two cardinal rules:

> As you rearrange, give the words the order you would probably give them in conversation with a friend.

> As you rearrange, do not omit any word, add any word, or change any word for another word.

Section A

Passage One (My Passage)

In the first court scene of *Hamlet,* Claudius formally announces his marriage to his former sister-in-law, Gertrude. As he makes his announcement, he breaks up a unit that resembles "had known," "will go," and "may think." That unit is "have taken" (I have italicized the words of this unit in the following passage):

> Therefore our sometime sister, now our queen,
> Th' imperial jointress to this warlike state,
> *Have* we, as 'twere with a defeated joy,
> With an auspicious and a dropping eye,
> With mirth in funeral and with dirge in marriage,
> In equal scale weighing delight and dole,
> *Taken* to wife.
> (1.2.8–14)

To give an ordinary, conversational arrangement to Claudius's words, I must, above all, move "Have" and "Taken" closer together. I can do so most easily if I move both "Have" and "Taken" much closer to the start of the clause, thus:

> Therefore we *have taken* to wife our sometime sister, now our queen, th' imperial jointress to this warlike state, as 'twere with a defeated joy, with an auspicious and a dropping eye, with mirth in funeral and with dirge in marriage, in equal scale weighing delight and dole.

Passage Two (Your Passage)

In *Hamlet,* the Ghost of Hamlet's murdered father reveals to Hamlet that the nation has been deceived by false explanations of his death. As he makes this declaration, the Ghost breaks up *a unit that resembles "was eaten" and "has been seen"*:

> So the whole ear of Denmark
> Is by a forgèd process of my death
> Rankly abused.
> (1.5.36–38)

Activities

● Present here the unit (the group of two or more related words) that the Ghost breaks up.

_____

- By rearranging the words of the Ghost's lines, put the separated parts of this unit closer together.

_____

_____

Passage Three (Your Passage)

Because the witches have convinced Macbeth that he bears "a charmèd life, which must not yield / To one of woman born" (5.8.12–13), Macbeth tells his enemy, Macduff, that he does not fear Macduff's sword. As he makes this assertion, Macbeth breaks up *a unit that resembles "may think"*:

> As easy mayst thou the intrenchant air
> With thy keen sword impress as make me bleed.
> (*Macbeth*, 5.8.9–10)

Activities

- Present here the unit (the group of two or more related words) that Macbeth breaks up.

_____

- By rearranging the words of Macbeth's lines, put the separated parts of this unit closer together.

_____

_____

Section B

Passage One (My Passage)

In the following lines from *Othello*, Iago is suggesting to Montano that Cassio is an unreliable officer. As Iago presents this suggestion, he breaks up a unit that resembles "water will run." The unit is "trust will shake." I have italicized the words of this unit in the following passage:

> I fear the *trust* Othello puts him in,
> On some odd time of his infirmity,
> *Will shake* this island.
>
> (2.3.120–22)

I can move "Will shake" and "trust" closer together by placing the last line ("Will shake this island") before the second line ("On some odd time of his infirmity"), thus:

> I fear the *trust* Othello puts him in *will shake* this island on some odd time of his infirmity.

Passage Two (Your Passage)

In the following lines from *King Lear* (where "aught" means "anything" and "like" means "please"), the enraged Lear presents his rejected daughter to the Duke of Burgundy as a thing of no value. As he does so, Lear breaks up *a unit that resembles "night may fall"*:

If aught within that little seeming substance,
Or all of it, with our displeasure pieced
And nothing more, may fitly like your Grace,
She's there, and she is yours.

(1.1.198–201)

Activities

- Present here the unit (the group of two or more related words) that Lear breaks up.

  _____

- By rearranging the words of Lear's lines, put the separated parts of this unit closer together.

  _____
  _____
  _____

Passage Three (Your Passage)

In *King Lear*, the blinded and guilt-ridden Duke of Gloucester dies in a moment of great emotion when he discovers that his son, Edgar, is with him. As Edgar describes his father's death, he breaks up *a unit that resembles "house burned"*:

But his flawed heart—
Alack, too weak the conflict to support—
'Twixt two extremes of passion, joy and grief,
Burst smilingly.

(5.3.197–200)

Activities

- Present here the unit (the group of two or more related words) that Edgar breaks up.

  _____

- By rearranging the words of Edgar's lines, put the separated parts of this unit closer together.

  _____
  _____
  _____

Passage Four (Your Passage)

In *Hamlet*, in an effort to shame his mother, Hamlet tells her to behave in an immoral fashion—in fact, to reveal to his principal enemy, Claudius, the secret that he is not mad, but sane. As he delivers his ironical message, Hamlet breaks up *a unit that resembles "council would decide"*:

'Twere good you let him know,
For who that's but a queen, fair, sober, wise,
Would from a paddock, from a bat, a gib,
Such dear concernings hide?

(3.4.189–92)

Activities

● Present here the unit (the group of two or more related words) that Hamlet breaks up.

_____

● By rearranging the words of Hamlet's lines, put the separated parts of this unit closer together.

_____

_____

_____

Section C

Passage One (My Passage)

In *The Winter's Tale,* as she refers to death as a mere "bug" (meaning "bugbear" or "bogey"), Queen Hermione tells her threatening husband, Leontes, that he can no longer frighten her. In making this declaration, Hermione breaks up two units that resemble "find the path" and "presents gold and silver." The units are "seek the bug" and "give crown and comfort." I have italicized the words of each unit in the following passage:

> Sir, spare your threats.
> *The bug* which you would fright me with I *seek.*
> To me can life be no commodity.
> The *crown and comfort* of my life, your favor,
> I do *give* lost, for I do feel it gone,
> But know not how it went.
>
> (3.2.90–95)

The following rearrangement shows how the separated words in Hermione's passage can be moved closer together.

> Sir, spare your threats. I *seek the bug* which you would fright me with. Life can
> be no commodity to me. I do *give* lost *the crown and comfort* of my life, your favor,
> for I do feel it gone, but know not how it went.

Passage Two (Your Passage)

In *Richard II,* as King Richard yields his authority to Bolingbroke and Northumberland, he bitterly says that Northumberland will never be satisfied with any share of the kingdom that Bolingbroke gives him. In making this statement, Richard breaks up *a unit that resembles "asked that I go" and "believe it is a lie."* (He also breaks up a unit that you should consider again as you are reading section D: a unit that resembles "you, walking in the sunlight.")

> Thou shalt think,
> Though he divide the realm and give thee half,
> It is too little, helping him to all.
>
> (5.1.59–61)

Activities

- Present here the unit (the group of two or more related words) that Richard breaks up.

  _____

- By rearranging the words of Richard's lines, put the separated parts of this unit closer together.

  _____

  _____

  _____

Section D

Passage One (My Passage)

In *King Lear*, as he sits alone in the stocks, Kent speaks of his need to sleep, and as he does so, he breaks up a unit that resembles "days long and humid." The unit is "eyes, all weary and o'erwatched" ("o'erwatched" eyes are eyes that have not closed in sleep for a long time); I have italicized the words of this unit in the following passage:

> *All weary and o'erwatched,*
> Take vantage, heavy *eyes*, not to behold
> This shameful lodging.
> (2.2.166–68)

One arrangement that puts Kent's separated words closer together is:

> Heavy *eyes, all weary and o'erwatched*, take vantage not to behold this shameful lodging.

Passage Two (Your Passage)

In *Hamlet*, Polonius tells his daughter, Ophelia, that she has been foolish to consider Prince Hamlet's "tenders" (or "offers") of affection to be "sterling" (that is, to be real rather than counterfeit). As Polonius makes this declaration, he breaks up *a unit that resembles "wonders that are present"*:

> Think yourself a baby
> That you have ta'en these tenders for true pay
> Which are not sterling.
> (1.3.105–7)

Activities

- Present here the unit (the group of two or more related words) that Polonius breaks up.

  _____

- By rearranging the words of Polonius's lines, put the separated parts of this unit closer together.

_____

_____

_____

Passage Three (Your Passage)

In *King Lear*, Edmund explains to Albany that he has put Lear and Lear's daughter, Cordelia, in confinement. As he speaks to Albany, Edmund breaks up *a unit that resembles "man whose horse broke free"*:

> Sir, I thought it fit
> To send the old and miserable King
> To some retention [and appointed guard];
> Whose age had charms in it, whose title more,
> To pluck the common bosom on his side
> And turn our impressed lances in our eyes . . . .
> (5.3.45–50)

Activities

- Present here the unit (the group of two or more related words) that Edmund breaks up.

_____

- By rearranging the words of Edmund's lines, put the separated parts of this unit closer together.

_____

_____

_____

See also "Passage Two" in section C.

Section E

Passage One (My Passage)

In *Othello*, after he is persuaded that Desdemona has been unfaithful, Othello often labors to convince himself that he is no longer softened by his love for her. As he makes such an effort in the following lines, he breaks up a unit that resembles "were sent away." The unit is "are blotted forth" (I have italicized the words of the unit in the following passage):

> *Forth* of my heart those charms, thine eyes, *are blotted*.
> (5.1.35)

To put the separated words closer together, I need only move "Forth of my heart" to the end:

> Those charms, thine eyes, *are blotted forth* of my heart.

Passage Two (Your Passage)

In *Julius Caesar*, Portia tries to persuade her husband, Brutus, to reveal the plans he and the other conspirators have made. As she speaks, she breaks up *a unit that resembles "is accepted inside the house"*:

> Within the bond of marriage, tell me, Brutus,
> Is it excepted I should know no secrets
> That appertain to you?
>
> > (2.1.280–82)

Activities

- Present here the unit (the group of two or more related words) that Portia breaks up.

  _____

- By rearranging the words of Portia's lines, put the separated parts of this unit closer together.

  _____

  _____

  _____

Reading Aloud

Read aloud the passages that you and I have created by rearranging words, and also read aloud the original lines from Shakespeare's plays. Use the familiar patterns of our arrangements to make yourself more comfortable with the unusual patterns of the more poetic lines.

WORKSHEET 6: IMITATING SHAKESPEARE—UNUSUAL SEQUENCES OF WORDS

Introduction

In worksheets 2 and 3, you considered Shakespearean clauses in which major elements appear in unusual sequences. In some, elements that would ordinarily come second came first, and in others, elements that would ordinarily come third came first. You can become more comfortable with such unexpected sequences in Shakespeare's clauses if you create such sequences in clauses of your own.

To begin such imitations of Shakespeare, you need to find, or make, sentences in which the major elements appear in expected, ordinary sequences. The following sentence is one that you could use. I have italicized the major elements in each of its two clauses:

> *He was pushing* the *cart* up the street by hand when the *wind carried* his *hat* away.

To form unusual sequences in revising this sentence, you would only need to change the order in which the major elements in each clause appear. You could have as one sequence, "cart was he pushing," and you could have as another sequence, "carried wind hat." The new version could be:

> The *cart* up the street by hand *was he pushing* when *carried* the *wind* his *hat* away.

Exercises

Exercise One

The following sentence provides two clauses that you can rearrange to create unusual sequences of major elements (I have italicized the major elements in each clause):

> Until that moment when *I heard* the *price* of it, *I had been favoring* the green *bag* over the red.

Activity

● In the blanks that follow, rearrange the words of the sentence just presented. In reshaping, be sure to change the positions of some of the italicized words. Do not add or omit any word, and do not change any word to another.

_____

_____

Exercise Two

Another sentence that you can change to produce unusual sequences is this one:

> As the *snow fell* over the rivers and *settled* among the trees, two *sparrows* sitting on an aspen's limb *considered* the thickening *air*.

Activity

● In the blanks that follow, rearrange the words of the sentence just provided. As you rearrange, change the positions of some of the major elements, which I have italicized. Do not add a word, omit a word, or change any word to another.

_____

_____

WORKSHEET 7: IMITATING SHAKESPEARE—SEPARATIONS OF RELATED PARTS

Introduction

In worksheet 5, you considered many passages in which Shakespearean characters separate related parts. To make such separations seem less strange, you can create similar separations in work of your own.

To form such separations, you must first find or make some writing in which the words are grouped in rather ordinary ways. The following sentence, for example, could provide material:

> Before I learned from a neighbor that the watering of lawns is strictly forbidden in August, I had watered the brown lawn, which was planted in July, for several hours.

After you have selected such a passage to revise, you should next mark a few of the most important units and then, by rearranging the words of the passage, break those units up. After starting with the sentence just presented, for instance, you could break up "I learned," "is strictly forbidden," and "had watered." The following is one sentence that you might produce by making such separations:

> Before I from a neighbor learned that of lawns the watering is in August strictly forbidden, I had the brown lawn, which in July planted was, for several hours watered.

Exercises

Exercise One

To imitate Shakespeare in the manner I have just described, start with the following sentence, and follow the directions provided after it:

> The copper Cadillac that *had seemed* to crawl languidly, like a spider, up the ragged blacktop *now rested* briefly at McKenzie's mill, and its *unwelcome, sun-chided pause* on this day preceding Easter *was a mortifying omen* for us all.

Activity

- In the blanks that follow, rearrange the words of the sentence just presented. As you do so, break up each of the italicized units (move at least one word in each unit away from another word in the unit). As you rearrange, do not add a word, omit a word, or change any word to another word.

_____

_____

_____

Exercise Two

The following statement provides additional material on which you can work to imitate Shakespeare:

I pledge allegiance to the flag of the United States of America, and to the republic for which it stands. . . .

Activity

- In the blanks that follow, rearrange the words of the statement just given. As you rearrange, separate related words, but do not add a word, omit a word, or change any word to another word.

_____

_____

WORKSHEET 8: IMITATING SHAKESPEARE—RHYMES, RHYTHMS, AND UNUSUAL ARRANGEMENTS

RHYMES

Introduction

Sometimes Shakespeare arranged words in unexpected ways because he wanted to put words that rhyme at the ends of his lines. Consider, for example, his arrangements in the following passage. These lines, from the final scene of *As You Like It,* Shakespeare meant to be spoken or sung (probably sung) by Hymen, god of marriage:

> Then is there mirth in heaven
> When earthly things made even
>   Atone together.
> Good Duke, receive thy daughter;
> Hymen from heaven brought her,
>   Yea, brought her hither,
> That thou mightst join her hand with his
> Whose heart within his bosom is.
>
> (5.4.102–9)

Note that each line rhymes with one other line (in Shakespeare's day, "heaven" rhymed with "even," "together" rhymed with "hither," "daughter" rhymed with "brought her," and "his" rhymed with "is." Note, too, that Shakespeare created some unusual sequences of words in order to put rhyming words at the ends of the lines. Instead of "Hymen brought her from heaven," we find "Hymen from heaven brought her," and instead of "is within his bosom," we find "within his bosom is."

An Example

To become more comfortable with Shakespeare's work—to make the processes that underlie that work more familiar—you, too, can arrange words in uncommon ways to create rhymes. First, create an ordinary sentence that includes two words that rhyme: a sentence such as "We have fun in June when the sun shines on flowers." Next, arrange the words of the sentence to form two lines, and put the rhyming words at the ends of the lines. For example, you might transform "We have fun in June when the sun shines on flowers" into:

> In June when shines the sun on flowers, we have fun.

Two Exercises

Exercise One

Another sentence on which you may practice is this one:

> The snow comes in January; wild winds blow, and the trees are bare.

Activity

- In the blanks that follow, arrange the words of the sentence just provided into two lines of poetry. Let the first line end with "snow" and the second line with "blow." As you rearrange, do not add, delete, or change any word.

	snow
	blow.

Exercise Two

For more practice in putting rhyming words at the ends of lines, start with the following collection of words:

> Then they did weep for sudden joy, and I sung for sorrow, that such a king should play bo-peep and go among the fools.

Activity

- From the sentence just provided, create four lines for a song. End the first line with "weep," the second with "sung," the third with "bo-peep," and the fourth with "among." As you rearrange the words to make these rhymes, do not add, delete, or change any word.

	weep
	sung
	bo-peep
	among.

To compare your result with the lines that Shakespeare constructed from these same words, see *King Lear*, 1.4.166–69.

POETIC RHYTHMS

Introduction

Shakespeare also arranged words in unexpected ways in order to create rhythmical lines. Particularly common are unusual arrangements that he created in order to produce lines of blank verse: unrhymed lines, each written with a standard line of ten syllables as a referent. Nearly all of the Shakespearean passages that you have seen in these eight worksheets are passages of blank verse.

Whenever he was writing blank verse, Shakespeare wrote with a background rhythm in mind, and in writing almost every line, he tried to produce a rhythm that was similar to, although not identical with, the background rhythm. This background rhythm results from a regular alternation of unstressed and stressed syllables. You can create this background rhythm by saying aloud the ten syllables that follow (stress each "DAH" as you read):

> da DAH da DAH da DAH da DAH da DAH

Since the background rhythm results from the careful placing of stresses, and since Shakespeare wanted to create a similar rhythm in nearly every line of blank verse, *he was usually very careful about the locations of his stressed syllables.* He usually did not want the stresses in a line to appear in locations greatly different from the locations that stresses have in the background rhythm. Consequently, *he often chose to avoid certain arrangements of syllables, and therefore, certain arrangements of words.*

For example, Shakespeare chose to avoid the following arrangements of words:

> And they bóre her úp awhíle mérmaid-líke.

This is a line that has a fairly ordinary arrangement of words, but it is a line that Shakespeare did *not* write. The stressed syllables—''bore,'' ''up,'' ''-while,'' ''mer-,'' and ''like''—appear in places too different from the places where the DAHs appear in ''da DAH da DAH da DAH da DAH da DAH.'' The following comparison will make the differences obvious:

and	they	BORE	her	UP	a-	WHILE	MER-	maid-	LIKE
da	DAH	da		DAH	da	DAH	da	DAH	da	DAH

As you can tell when you amplify the emphases on ''bore,'' ''up,'' ''-while,'' ''mer-,'' and ''like'' and try to move with the line, the line has no rhythmical character. We could not dance to it.

So, instead of writing that line, Shakespeare created one, for *Hamlet*, in which the words have a rather unusual arrangement. That line is:

> And mermaid-like awhile they bore her up. . . .
> (4.7.175)

The stresses here *do* create a satisfactory pattern. Again, a comparison will be useful.

and	MER-	maid-	LIKE	a-	WHILE	they	BORE	her	UP
da	DAH	da	DAH	da	DAH	da	DAH	da	DAH

Clearly, this line, with its peculiar arrangement of words, does have rhythmical character. We could dance to it much more easily than we could dance to the line that Shakespeare did *not* write.

Exercise

To help you try your hand at forming lines of blank verse, I have presented, in the following activity, four more lines that Shakespeare did *not* write.

Activity

- Rearrange the words of each of the four lines below. As you do so, create a pattern of stressed and unstressed syllables that resembles ''da DAH da DAH da DAH da DAH da DAH.'' *In each line, I have italicized the word or words that you need to move in order to create a rhythmical sequence of syllables. As you rearrange, do* not add any word, omit any word, or change any word to another word. *Note that as you make each line more poetic, you also make the arrangement of its words less ordinary, more strange.* Write your new arrangement for each line in the blank that follows the line.

  If such calms *come after every tempest*

  _____

  Now confusion hath made his masterpiece

  _____

Let all the battlements *fire* their ordnance

But soft! What light *breaks* through yonder window?

To compare your creations with the lines that Shakespeare himself composed, see: *Othello,* 2.1.183; *Macbeth,* 2.3.62; *Hamlet,* 5.2.259; and *Romeo and Juliet,* 2.2.2.

SECTION 2: SHAKESPEARE'S TROUBLESOME OMISSIONS—THREE WORKSHEETS FOR THE CLASSROOM

Introduction

Almost all of the omissions produced by Shakespeare's characters develop from schemes that we and our students frequently use and observe. As readers in the classroom, however, students often find the omissions in the speeches of Shakespeare's characters to be disturbing, or even baffling. For three main reasons, they cannot adequately use the practices of the twentieth century to understand the practices of the past.

First, when students produce their own omissions and respond to those produced by others, they usually do so, not consciously, but unconsciously. Second, they usually do so not as writers and readers, but as speakers and hearers. Third, being reluctant to intrude on great literature, students are reluctant to add mentally to the speeches of Shakespeare's characters as boldly as they add to the speeches they hear in conversation. Thus, to help students improve in their responses to Shakespearean omissions, the teacher must perform three fundamental tasks:

1. The teacher must help the students perceive the omissions that occur in ordinary modern conversations.

2. The teacher must help the students link omissions in Shakespearean speeches with common modern omissions.

3. The teacher must encourage the students to contribute at times to Shakespearean speeches even as they take them in.

In preparing the three worksheets for this section, I have kept these three tasks in mind. In the first worksheet, I have demonstrated for the students that they often omit both syllables and parts of syllables as they talk. I have also presented shortened words and syllables from Shakespeare's plays, and I have invited the students to use some of those in original sentences.

In the second worksheet, which treats omissions of words, I have once more mixed citations from Shakespeare with modern examples. Each of the five sections in the worksheet includes two or three passages from Shakespeare, and each has four statements in modern English to introduce those passages. In addition, I have urged the students to read *aloud* not only the modern statements but also the Shakespearean statements. Only by reading aloud can they adequately experience the connections between Shakespeare's language and their own.

In the third and last worksheet, I have asked the students to create sentences from which they can remove words similar to the words omitted by Shakespearean characters, and I have asked them to put the removable words in brackets. To provide examples, I have carried over, from worksheet 2, ten statements that present such removable words in brackets. Five are modern statements and five are Shakespearean statements to which I have made additions.

While attending to the main tasks already mentioned, I have also tried to provide a truly introductory selection of Shakespearean omissions. In worksheet 1, I have presented words with syllables missing from various locations. Then, in worksheet 2, I have shown sentences that are missing words of five main kinds. The speakers in sections A, B, C, and E of that worksheet omit prepositions, predicates, subjects, and both subjects and predicates that most modern readers would expect to find. The speakers in section D omit words whose meanings they create implicitly by uses of the subjunctive mood.

Furthermore, in preparing these worksheets, I have tried to lead the students forward in easy steps. Thus, I have arranged the omissions in worksheets 1 and 2 so that students can gradually move from some that are easy to understand to others that are much more difficult. Also, in worksheet 2, as in the worksheets on arrangements, I have provided the students with models. In each section, I have taken at least one Shakespearean passage as my own and have marked at least one place in it. I have also given a word or words that I could insert at each place to make the passage clearer. I have then asked the students to respond to a similar passage with one or both of the same activities.

In ending, I can mention an exercise that I have not presented in the worksheets but enthusi-astically recommend. The directions read as follows:

> Write three pages of sustained dialogue for two speakers who are near you in age and who live in a place very much like your hometown. Study the dialogue for omissions of words, syllables, and parts of syllables. Then compare the omissions that occur in your dialogue with those that appear in the speeches of Shakespeare's characters.

Through this exercise, students can intensify the associations to which the following worksheets contribute—associations between the spoken, living English of their own world and the spoken, living English of Shakespeare's plays.

WORKSHEET 1: OMISSIONS OF SYLLABLES AND PARTS OF SYLLABLES

Part A

Often when we speak we reduce syllables: we leave out sounds that we usually include when we are speaking formally and carefully. For example, we change "to" to "t'," "be" to "b'," "with" to "wi'," "-ing" to "-in'," "let" to "le'," "that" to "tha'," "you" to "ya," and "here" to "'ere." We do so in such statements as:

> I'm goin' t' town.
> Tha's good—lemme go wi' ya.
> I'll b' darned if you are.
> C'mere.

Shakespeare's characters also compress syllables. They commonly change:

> "on" and "of" to "o'"
> "in" to "i'"
> "the" to "th'"

They do so in such phrases as "o' fire" (for "on fire"), "o' poison" (for "of poison"), and "i' th' orchard" (for "in the orchard").
Shakespeare's characters also make such reductions as:

> "it" to "'t"
> "he" to "'a"
> "be" to "b'"
> "with" to "wi'"
> "them" to "'em"
> "have" to "ha'" or "'a'"

Such reductions appear in phrases like "God b' wi' you," "God 'a' mercy on his soul," "They say 'a made a good end," "'T may, I grant," and "Will you ha' the truth on't."
Because you make compressions in your everyday life that are similar to the compressions that appear in Shakespeare's plays, you should be able to adjust rather easily to those made by Shakespeare's characters. You can accelerate your adjustment, however, by forming in original sentences compressions to match some of those in the plays. The following section will give you the opportunity to form such compressions.

Activity

- In the following spaces write eight *short* sentences. In each sentence use the compressed form specified in the preceding direction.
  Use "o'" for "on."

  _____

  Use "o'" for "of."

  _____

  Use "i'" for "in."

  _____

Use "'t" for "it."

Use "b'" for "be."

Use "wi'" for "with."

Use "'em" for "them."

Use "ha'" for "have."

Part B

As we often omit parts of syllables when we speak, so we often omit entire syllables. For example, when I say "I'd" (for "I would"), I change two syllables into one syllable. Likewise, I change two syllables into one when I say "I'm" (for "I am") or "he's" (for "he is"). In addition, I omit syllables in such expressions as "intemp'rate weather," "t'upper Wisconsin," "Heav'n forbid!", and "Don't just pour't down."

Shakespeare's characters also omit syllables often. Sometimes they omit syllables by altering the beginnings of words, sometimes by altering the middle parts of words, and sometimes by altering the endings of words. For example, we find:

"be't" (for "be it")
"between's" (for "between us")
"'bout" (for "about")
"do't" (for "do it")
"'tis" (for "it is")
"thou'dst" (for "thou wouldst")
"'mongst" (for "amongst")
"'twill" (for "it will")
"hear't" (for "hear it")
"on's" (for "on us")
"shall't" (for "shall it")
"thou'rt" (for "thou art")

"be'st" (for "beest")
"ling'ring" (for "lingering")
"ord'ring" (for "ordering")
"med'cine" (for "medicine")
"sland'rous" (for "slanderous")
"high'st" (for "highest")
"ta'en" (for "taken")
"whe'r" (for "whether")
"e'er" (for "ever")
"ne'er" (for "never")
"mak'st" (for "makest")

"t'untie" (for "to untie")
"t'have" (for "to have")

Also, characters in Shakespeare's plays sometimes reduce "God's" to "z" or "s" and then merge the "z" or "s" with another syllable. We find, for example, both "Zounds" and " 'Swounds" for "God's wounds." We also find " 'Sblood" for "God's blood" and " 'Slight" for "God's light." Because such oaths are always important—and particularly so in plays that are rich in religious allusions—we must remind ourselves that "God's," partially heard in such phrases, is implicitly present in them.

Furthermore, Shakespeare's characters sometimes omit one particularly important syllable from words where we would expect that syllable to be present as an ending. That syllable is "-ly." We find, for example, "I will speak as *liberal* as the north" (*Othello*, 5.2.221) and "What you will have, I'll give, and *willing* too" (*Richard II*, 3.3.206). We would say liberal*ly*," not "liberal," and willing*ly*," not "willing."

Just as you can accelerate your adjustment to Shakespeare's language by imitating his characters in forming compressions, so you can accelerate your adjustment by imitating his characters in omitting syllables. In the activity section that follows, you will find space and directions for this sort of imitation.

Activity

● In the following spaces, write eight short sentences. In each sentence use the abbreviated form or combination specified in the preceding direction.

Use "y'are" for "you are."

_____

Use "t'open" for "to open."

_____

Use "e'er" for "ever."

_____

Use "stol'n" for "stolen."

_____

Use "ta'en" for "taken."

_____

Use "on's" for "on us."

_____

Use "e'en" for "even."

_____

Use "late" for "lately."

_____

WORKSHEET 2: OMISSIONS OF
WORDS

Introduction

When you and I talk, we sometimes omit not only syllables and parts of syllables, but also words—words that would make our meanings clearer if we included them. Also, we expect our hearers to supply mentally the omitted words or some similar words. Thus, we force our hearers to participate with us in order to understand us.

The five statements that follow provide some examples. Each of these statements includes a word or words that you or I might well omit while talking. I have put the words that we might omit in brackets. *Read each sentence aloud twice. In your first reading, INCLUDE the bracketed word or words. In the second reading, OMIT the bracketed word or words. Be sure to read ALOUD!*

1. Yeah, you're right. We do need his help, and I've already written [to] him about it.
2. If that call's for me, [say] I'm not at home.
3. That ball of string—where is it? Darn! [It] was here just a minute ago.
4. [If you] do that to me again, Jack, I'll throw this dirty water in your face—so help me!
5. No way! that first song didn't get to me nearly so much, not nearly, as the second, and—wait a minute, now, I don't care what you say—[that song didn't get to] the rest of the audience either.

Such sentences as these can help you prepare to read Shakespeare's plays. In Shakespeare's plays, as in our own everyday world, speakers sometimes omit words from their sentences, and when they do, they expect their hearers to supply mentally some words to replace the ones omitted. And since we are hearers for Shakespeare's speakers, we must sometimes contribute words to their statements. We must add, we must intrude, we must participate. Otherwise, we can never adequately understand.

Fortunately, the five major kinds of omissions that appear in the speeches of Shakespeare's characters are not strange to us. In fact, while reading the preceding five statements—the ones with bracketed words—you produced omissions of all five kinds. Now, by working through the five sections that follow (sections A through E), you can use your understanding of these five statements to develop an understanding of similar statements from Shakespeare's plays.

Each of the five sections (A through E) begins with one of the five statements you have already seen and with three statements similar to it. These introductory statements contain bracketed words that you should first include, then omit, as you read aloud. The statements in each section are similar because the bracketed words in them resemble one another.

After the introductory statements in each section come two (or, in one section, three) passages from Shakespeare. In these passages, Shakespearean speakers omit words that are similar to the words bracketed in the four introductory statements. By moving from the modern statements to the Shakespearean statements, you will be using the familiar to draw close to the strange.

Of the two or three Shakespearean passages in each section, I have made myself responsible for all but the last. The last in each section is yours. In working with each of my passages, I have inserted at least one *X* within the speaker's lines. Each *X* marks a spot where the speaker has not included some word or words that I can provide to make the statement clearer. Also, in responding to each passage, I have given the word or words that I might add mentally at each *X*. I have asked you to work with your passage in each section in much the same way.

As you work with each of your Shakespearean passages, do not be afraid to guess at—to conjecture about—the character's meaning. Sometimes, we can do nothing more. And do not hesitate to add words mentally simply because Shakespeare is Shakespeare. You are working here with lively, flesh-and-blood dialogue, not with something cold, removed, and sacred.

You can accelerate your progress by reading aloud not only the modern statements, but also the Shakespearean statements. You need to force yourself to connect Shakespeare's English with the English of your own conversations. Reading aloud is the way!

Section A

Four Modern English Statements

Read aloud twice each of the following statements. In your first reading, include the word enclosed in brackets. In the second reading, omit the bracketed word. After you have read all four statements, try to understand how each bracketed word resembles every other bracketed word.

> Yeah, you're right. We do need his help, and I've already written [to] him about it.

> Well, I really don't know how to answer. [During] that week everything was kind of foggy.

> Listen, I threw [at] them all the insults I could think of.

> Please, Huey, do [for] me just one little favor.

Passage One (My Passage)

In *A Midsummer Night's Dream*, Nick Bottom wants to play the lion in a drama that he and some friends will perform, and in the following remarks, he tells his fellows that he will not roar too fearfully if given that role. As he speaks, Bottom omits a word that you and I would surely include:

> I grant you, friends, if you should fright the
> ladies out of their wits, they would have no more
> discretion but to hang us; but I will aggravate my voice so
> that I will roar   X   you as gently as any sucking dove. . . .
> (1.2.72–75)

Bottom's construction in "roar you as gently" is similar to the one you produced when you left out the bracketed word in "do [for] me just one little favor." Further, the word we can most easily add at the *X* to make the passage clearer is the same one you omitted: "for." Thus, we can understand Bottom's "roar you as gently as any sucking dove" to mean, "roar [for] you as gently as any sucking dove."

Passage Two (Your Passage)

In the next to last act of *Hamlet,* Gertrude reports the manner of Ophelia's death. As she makes this report, Gertrude, like Bottom, omits a word that you or I would probably include. She says of Ophelia:

> Her clothes spread wide,
> And mermaid-like awhile they bore her up,
> Which time she chanted snatches of old lauds,
> As one incapable of her own distress. . . .
>   (4.7.174–77)

Activity

- First, read again the second introductory statement for this section (the one that includes " [During] that week everything was kind of foggy"). Next, put a large X at that place where Gertrude does not include a word that you or I probably would include.

  Now write in the following blank a word that you could insert at the X to make the passage clearer. The word should be "during," "at," "in," or some similar word.

  _____

Section B

Four Modern English Statements

Read aloud twice each of the following statements. First include, then omit, the word or words enclosed in brackets. After you have read all four statements, try to understand how each bracketed word or set of words resembles every other bracketed word or set of words.

> If that call's for me, [say] I'm not at home.

> Please, [close] the door!

> I've already told you. He should stay there, you [should stay] here.

> I did it, whether they liked it or not. They thought I would just keep myself locked up in this stupid room and [would keep] you [locked] away from me. But I won't! I won't!

Passage One (My Passage)

In *As You Like It,* the loyal old servant, Adam, offers to his young master, Orlando, all the money that he has saved for his declining years. As Adam makes this offer, he omits some words that you or I would probably include. Adam says:

> I have five hundred crowns,
> The thrifty hire I saved under your father,
> Which I did store to be my foster nurse
> When service should in my old limbs lie lame
> And unregarded age   X   in corners thrown.
>   (2.3.38–42)

The construction that Adam forms here resembles the constructions you made when omitting "should stay" and "would keep . . . locked" from the third and fourth preceding statements. The words that Adam omits are "should" and "lie." He expects Orlando to carry those two words over from the fourth line and supply them mentally in the last line. He expects Orlando to understand his meaning to be:

> I have five hundred crowns,
> The thrifty hire I saved under your father,
> Which I did store to be my foster nurse
> When service should in my old limbs lie lame
> And unregarded age [should lie] in corners thrown.

Passage Two (Your Passage)

In the opening act of *Twelfth Night*, Maria tells Olivia that a caller is at her gate. Olivia suspects that the caller represents the Count Orsino, who has been pleading for her love. Since Olivia does not want to hear more of Count Orsino's messages, she instructs Malvolio to keep the caller away from her. She tells him:

> If it be a suit from the Count, I am sick, or not at home.
> What you will, to dismiss it.
>
>   (1.5.103–4)

Activity

- First, consider again the first of the preceding four statements: "If that call's for me, [say] I'm not at home." Next, place a large *X* at each place where Olivia has not included a word that we probably would include. Number each *X*.

  Now write in the following blanks the words that you could insert at your two marks to make the passage clearer.

  _____   _____

Section C

Four Modern English Statements

Read aloud twice each of the following statements. First include, then omit, the word or words enclosed in brackets. After you have read all four statements, try to understand how each bracketed word or set of words resembles every other bracketed word or set of words.

That ball of string—where is it? Darn! [It] was here just a minute ago.

What did he do? [He] hit a tree with the mower, that's what. And [he] broke the lawn rake.

I'm not sorry. [To be] sorry is [to be] stupid, and I'm not stupid.

She's nosy, she's noisy . . . [she] brings in bags of stinking onions . . . and [she] should be kicked out, as soon as possible—that's what I think.

Passage One (My Passage)

In the central scene of *Othello,* Iago talks to Othello about the pain valuable possessions may cause. One who has such possessions and yet fears their loss, says Iago, is forever miserable. As he makes this declaration, Iago twice omits words that you or I would probably include. His statement is:

> X Poor and content is X rich, and rich enough;
> But riches fineless is as poor as winter
> To him that ever fears he shall be poor.
> (3.3.172–74)

Iago's statement is similar to the third statement given above (the one that includes, " [To be] sorry is [to be] stupid"). Although we cannot be absolutely certain of Iago's meaning, one way of making his statement clearer is to add "to be" or "being" at each place where I have put an X. Filled out with such additions, the statement would read, " [Being] Poor and content is [being] rich" or " [To be] Poor and content is [to be] rich."

Passage Two (Your Passage)

In *Twelfth Night,* after a fight with Sebastian, Sir Andrew Aguecheek appears on stage in great distress, crying "For the love of God, a surgeon!" When Olivia asks him "What's the matter?" Andrew replies with such passion that he twice omits a word that his hearers must supply. Says Andrew:

> Has broke my head across, and has given
> Sir Toby a bloody coxcomb too.
> (5.1.169-70)

Activity

- First, consider again the second of the four preceding statements (the one that includes "[He] hit a tree" and "[he] broke the lawn rake"). Next, put a large X at each place in the passage where Andrew has omitted a word that we would ordinarily include in such a statement. Number each X.

  Now write in the following blanks the words that you could insert at your two marks to make the passage clearer.

  _____   _____

Section D

Four Modern English Statements

Read aloud twice each of the following statements. First include, then omit, the word or words enclosed in brackets. After you have read all four statements, try to understand how each bracketed word or set of words resembles every other bracketed word or set of words.

> [If you] do that to me again, Jack, I'll throw this dirty water in your face—so help me!

I'll tell you what . . . [if] you go home, that's it—finished, the end, forever.

If you make it to bed tonight, [may you] sleep well.

Yeah, I heard you say he wants to talk to me. If it'll make him feel better, [let him] talk to me as much as he likes . . . but it won't do him any good—not at all. I promise you.

Passage One (My Passage)

In *Richard III*, the Duchess of York bids farewell to her murderous son, Richard, by wishing him defeat in a coming battle. As she pronounces this curse, the Duchess twice omits a word that we would probably include:

> X My prayers on the adverse party fight,
> And   X   there the little souls of Edward's children
> Whisper the spirits of thine enemies
> And promise them success and victory!
> (4.4.191–94)

The Duchess's statement resembles the one you created when you omitted the bracketed words in " [may you] sleep well." Although we do not need to imagine a "you" for her statement, we do need to imagine a "may" for the first line and another "may" for the second. Thus, filling out her statement, we might think it to mean:

> [May] My prayers on the adverse party fight,
> And [may] there the little souls of Edward's children
> Whisper the spirits of thine enemies
> And promise them success and victory!

Passage Two (Your Passage)

In *Julius Caesar*, as he greets the conspirators who have killed Caesar, Antony tells them that he is willing to be killed, also, if they intend to take his life. As he makes this declaration, Antony omits two words that you or I would probably include. He tells the others:

> Live a thousand years,
> I shall not find myself so apt to die;
> No place will please me so, no mean of death,
> As here by Caesar, and by you cut off. . . .
> (3.1.159–62)

Activity

- First, as you consider again the first two statements given for this section (those that include "[If you] do that" and "[if] you go"), think about the meaning of "Live a thousand years." Next, put a large *X* at that place in the passage where Antony has omitted words that we would ordinarily include in such a statement.

  Now, in the following blank, write the words that you could insert at the *X* to make the passage clearer.

  _____

Section E

Four Modern English Statements

Read aloud twice each of the following statements. First include, then omit, the word or words enclosed in brackets. After you have read all four statements, try to understand how each set of bracketed words resembles every other set.

> No way! That first song didn't get to me nearly so much, not nearly, as the second, and—wait a minute, now, I don't care what you say—[that song didn't get to] the rest of the audience either.

> Where do you think he was? [He was] at home. [He was] working on his car. [He was] in the swimming pool. That's where.

> I like ice cream a lot, and, every now and then, [I] also . . . [like] putting fruit on top of it.

> I don't care what you decide, Rebecca! If you want brown shoes, fine! Or if [you want] . . . I don't know, lavender with pink polka dots, that's fine, too. Just let's get out of here!

Passage One (My Passage)

In the second act of *Othello*, Othello angrily asks Iago to tell him how a disruptive fight between Cassio and Montano began. In replying, Iago on three occasions omits words that you or I would probably include in such a statement. He tells Othello:

> I do not know. X Friends all, but now, even now,
> In quarter, and in terms like bride and groom
> Devesting them for bed; and then, but now—
> As if some planet had unwitted men—
> X Swords out, and X tilting one at other's breast
> In opposition bloody.
> (2.3.169–74)

Iago's constructions resemble the ones you created when you omitted the bracketed words in: "[He was] at home. [He was] working on his car. [He was] in the swimming pool." Thus we can imagine some words similar to "He was" at each *X*. The best choices for me are "They were," "They had," and "they were." Consequently, when I fill the lines out mentally, they mean:

> I do not know. [They were] Friends all, but now, even now,
> In quarter, and in terms like bride and groom
> Devesting them for bed; and then, but now—
> As if some planet had unwitted men—
> [They had] Swords out, and [they were] tilting one at other's breast
> In opposition bloody.

Passage Two (My Passage)

In *The Winter's Tale*, Florizel, Prince of Bohemia, has dressed himself in the clothes of a country fellow so that he can be near Perdita, a woman whom he believes to be a mere shepherdess. In the following lines, Florizel compares himself with a number of deities who changed themselves into lower creatures so that they could be with mortal women. He says the deities sought no greater beauty than he is seeking, and he says his change came from motives superior to theirs:

> Their transformations
> Were never for a piece of beauty rarer,
> Nor   X   in a way so chaste, since my desires
> Run not before mine honor, nor my lusts
> Burn hotter than my faith.
>
> (4.4.31–35)

In making this statement, Florizel expects Perdita to supply some words mentally at the place where I have put the X. These words, which he expects her to carry over from the first two lines, are "their," "were," and "transformations." He expects her to understand his statement to mean:

> Their transformations
> Were never for a piece of beauty rarer,
> Nor [were their transformations] in a way so chaste, since my desires
> Run not before mine honor, nor my lusts
> Burn hotter than my faith.

Passage Three (Your Passage)

In *The Tempest*, Prince Ferdinand wants to convince Miranda that he truly loves her. Thus, he responds to her "Do you love me?" by strongly protesting his sincerity. As he does so, he omits two words that you and I would probably include. He says:

> O heaven, O earth, bear witness to this sound,
> And crown what I profess with kind event
> If I speak true! if hollowly, invert
> What best is boded me to mischief!
>
> (3.1.68–71)

Activity

- In the blanks that follow, write two words that you can add between "if" and "hollowly" to make Ferdinand's statement clearer. Choose two words that Ferdinand has already used.

_____   _____

WORKSHEET 3: IMITATING
SHAKESPEARE

In worksheet 2, I presented five groups of sentences written in modern English. In those sentences, I put in brackets the kinds of words that Shakespearean characters are likely to omit. Furthermore, to some passages from Shakespeare's plays, I added words that helped me understand the speakers' meanings. These additional words I also put in brackets.

Now I have quoted again, in pairs, five of my modern sentences and also five Shakespearean statements. After each pair, I have left a space for you to create a statement of your own—a statement similar to either one or both of the statements given. The places for your statements are marked by bullets.

As you compose each of your statements, you should enclose in brackets a word or words that you can either include or omit. *Also, you should read aloud twice each of your statements, first including, then omitting, the word or words you have put in brackets.* By composing and reading such statements, you can help yourself become comfortable with similar statements in Shakespeare's works.

Section A

Please, Huey, do [for] me just one little favor.

but I will aggravate my voice so that I will roar [for] you
as gently as any sucking dove. . . .

● _____

_____

Section B

They thought I would just keep myself locked up in this stupid room and [would keep] you [locked] away from me. But I won't! I won't!

I have five hundred crowns,
The thrifty hire I saved under your father,
Which I did store to be my foster nurse
When service should in my old limbs lie lame
And unregarded age [should lie] in corners thrown.

● _____

_____

Section C

[To be] sorry is [to be] stupid, and I'm not stupid.

[To be] Poor and content is [to be] rich,
    and rich enough. . . .

● _____

_____

Section D

If you make it to bed tonight, [may you] sleep well.

[May] My prayers on the adverse party fight. . . .

● _____

_____

Section E

I like ice cream a lot, and, every now and then, [I] also . . . [like] putting fruit on top of it.

> Their transformations
> Were never for a piece of beauty rarer,
> Nor [were their transformations] in a way so chaste. . . .

● _____

_____

SECTION 3: WORDS NOT QUITE OUR OWN

Introduction

A few strange words appear in Shakespeare's plays often enough, or in such significant positions, that they cause notable disturbances for modern readers. Chief among these are:

ague	cuckold	methinks
anon	fain	moe
arras	hap	moiety
ay	haply	prithee
betimes	hest	sirrah
choler	hie	withal
cozen	maugre	

In addition, a number of words have so changed in their spellings that they appear to us to be words we do not know. Examples are "corse," "lanthorn," and "hautboy," the equivalents of "corpse," "lantern," and "oboe."

Still, the words that most frequently trouble readers of Shakespeare are words that readers think they know well—common words that have shifted, or grown, or shrunk in their meanings since the early seventeenth century. Therefore I have concentrated on such words in this final section.

I have presented one hundred and twelve words of this sort in all. These are words that appear in some of Shakespeare's best known scenes, and nearly all are words I found glossed repeatedly in modern editions of twenty well-known plays. Also, using information presented by the standard reference works (particularly Murray 1933, Schmidt 1962, and Onions 1986), I have provided the most important of the words' unexpected meanings. Furthermore, to assist teachers and students who want to start with a smaller collection of words, I have marked with bullets thirty to which readers of Shakespeare should give special attention.

As I indicated in the theory and research section, I have presented the words of section 3 in contexts of two different kinds. First, I have shown each word at work in at least one sentence, or part of a sentence, from one of Shakespeare's plays. Second, I have put each word with another word or with two or several words that are related to it in meaning or function. For example, I have placed in one group words that concern time and relationships in time; in another, words that concern openness, revelation, and secrecy; and in another, words that function as auxiliary verbs (words that assist). Such groupings can enable students to perceive individual words as significant parts of important verbal networks.

To make fully appropriate use of these materials, teachers will have to provide assignments that allow students to concentrate on, and to take charge of, a few selected words. Especially helpful are assignments that allow the students to create new groups and to use words in original compositions (Carr and Wixson 1985/86; Stahl 1985/86). The assignments that follow will serve as examples. All may be used with the collection of words, meanings, and passages that follow or with some similar collection.

Assignment A: Selecting Words for a Report or Letter

The attached collection includes one hundred and twelve familiar words that sometimes or always appear with unexpected meanings in Shakespeare's plays. Select from these at least ten words that you could use in a love letter; or select ten that you could use to report the events of a particularly bad day. Write beside each of your words the unexpected meaning you would want it to have in your letter or report.

Assignment B: Using Words in a Poem

Write a poem about some sixteenth-century figure (a young boy in rural England, for example, or the daughter of a great nobleman, or a shoemaker's wife in London). Imagine the person in some specific location (for instance, beside a river, in a formal garden, or in a crowded street). As you write the poem, use some words from the attached collection—at least seven—with meanings that are Shakespearean but not modern.

Assignment C: Using Words in a Skit

Preparation

Choose a partner and with that partner select ten of the one hundred and twelve words given in the attached collection.

Composition

In collaboration with your partner, write five or six pages of dialogue. In this dialogue, use your ten special words with meanings that they sometimes or always have for Shakespeare's characters but do not have for us in the twentieth century. In such a dialogue, you might, for example, use "an" to mean "if"; "for" to mean "because"; "or" to mean "either"; "still" to mean "forever"; "abuse" to mean "deceive"; "honest" to mean "respectable"; and "blood" to mean "passion." In composing your dialogue, feel free to create a dramatic situation similar to one used often in the various comedies, melodramatic "soaps," or adventure series that appear on television. (You may create, if you wish, a parody of an episode you have seen on television.)

Performance

Use your dialogue to create a three- or four-minute performance before the class. You may read the dialogue aloud while creating appropriate movements and gestures. You may memorize your entire script and then perform it. Or, finally, you may memorize just parts of your script and use those parts as the basic elements in an im-provised performance. But do not identify your special words for the members of your audience. Instead, instruct those in the audience to identify those words themselves and to write them down as they hear you use them in your dialogue.

Discussion

After your performance, ask the members of your audience to name the words you have used in unexpected ways, and ask them to give the meanings you intended those words to have.

Assignment D: Using Words in Sentences That Might Appear in Popular Songs

Consider the thirty words in the following collection that have bullets beside them (the words are "still," "straight," "success," "but," "an," "or," "nor," "fancy," "affect," "kind," "blood," "prove," "mere," "brave," "like," "sad," "honest," "jealous," "doubt," "humor," "mischief," "abuse," "envy," "toy," "part," "owe," "grace," "discover," "will," and "would"). Choose ten of those words and use each of the ten in one sentence (write ten sentences in all). Use each word with a meaning that is Shakespearean but not modern. Let each sentence be a statement, a question, an exclamation, or a command that might appear in a popular song. Be prepared to sing your sentences for your classmates.

A Note to Teachers

Teachers who use assignments A, B, and D can make them more valuable by giving students opportunities to share their lists and compositions with others, and teachers can make all four assignments more valuable by participating with students in the required activities. By joining the students in their verbal games and by allowing them to share written productions, teachers implicitly urge their students to transform troublesome Shakespearean words into expressive devices—to make them not only objects of study, but also personal possessions fit to be used in spirited social play.

FAMILIAR WORDS WITH UNEXPECTED MEANINGS: AN INITIAL COLLECTION

The meanings of words can change over time. In Shakespeare's plays, many still common words appear with meanings quite different from the meanings that they ordinarily have in the twentieth century. Such words can be like the flaming spirits that Caliban speaks of in *The Tempest*. They can lead you "like a firebrand, in the dark" out of your way and leave you weary and confused (2.2.6).

To help you avoid the misunderstandings that these difficult words can cause, I have introduced more than one hundred of them in the following pages, and I have presented with these words the most troublesome meanings that they can carry. I have also marked with bullets thirty of these words to which you should give special attention. All thirty are words that appear numerous times and in important episodes in Shakespeare's plays.

In addition, I have organized the words into twenty groups. Within each group the words connect with one another through their meanings or through their functions.

After you have considered all of these words, you can use some of them with their unexpected meanings in original compositions. Or you can imagine that you are writing letters, poems, dramas, or reports and can choose words that you might use with unexpected meanings in each piece. Through such activities you can make the unexpected meanings of the words important to you personally and so, make them memorable.

Group A: Words That Concern Time and Relationships in Time

A.1. *SOFT.* "Soft" may mean "slowly now" or "gently," and it sometimes appears where a modern speaker might use "Wait a minute" or "Hold on." Thus, Hamlet interrupts himself with that word when he realizes Ophelia is nearby:

> Soft you now,
> The fair Ophelia!—Nymph, in thy orisons
> Be all my sins remembered.
>
> (*Hamlet*, 3.1.88–90)

● A.2. *STILL.* "Still" often means "always," "ever," "continually," or "constantly." So, in *A Midsummer Night's Dream*, Oberon means that Puck is either always blundering or always causing problems intentionally when he tells him:

> Still thou mistak'st,
> Or else committ'st thy knaveries willfully.
> (3.2.345–46)

● A.3. *STRAIGHT.* "Straight" often means "straightaway," "immediately."

> This will I tell my lady straight

says Feste (*Twelfth Night*, 4.1.27), after he sees Toby start a fight with Sebastian.

A.4. *PRESENT.* "Present" often means "immediate," and though "presently" may mean "by and by," it usually means "immediately" or "instantly." The Countess in *All's Well That Ends Well* tells the Clown:

> give Helen this,
> And urge her to a present answer back.
>
> (2.2.57–58)

Paulina tells those gathered to see the statue:

> Either forbear,
> Quit presently the chapel, or resolve you
> For more amazement.
>
> (*The Winter's Tale*, 5.3.85–87)

A.5. *TO-NIGHT.* "To-night" may mean "last night." Just before he is murdered by the plebeians, Cinna the Poet says:

> I dreamt to-night that I did feast with Caesar,
> And things unluckily charge my fantasy.
>
> (*Julius Caesar*, 3.3.1–2)

A.6. *SINCE.* "Since" may mean "when," "when in the past," or "ago." Florizel, who is twenty-one, asks Leontes, who is forty-four, to recall the time when he was in love:

> Beseech you, sir,
> Remember since you owed no more to time
> Than I do now. With thought of such affections,
> Step forth mine advocate.
>
> (*The Winter's Tale*, 5.1.217–20)

A.7. *PREVENT.* "Prevent" may mean "come before," "anticipate," "hinder in advance," or "forestall." Hamlet says to Rosencrantz and Guildenstern that he will himself tell why they were sent for:

> So shall my anticipation prevent your
> discovery, and your secrecy to the king
> and queen moult no feather.
>
> (*Hamlet*, 2.2.290–92)

• A.8. *SUCCESS.* "Succeed" usually means "follow" or "come to pass," and "success" often means just "outcome" or "issue." In *All's Well That Ends Well*, Parolles promises Bertram that he will try to recover their drum:

> I know not what the success will be, my lord,
> but the attempt I vow.
>
> (3.6.72–73)

Othello, having found Desdemona safe after a storm at sea, says he doubts that:

> another comfort like to this
> Succeeds in unknown fate.
>
> (*Othello*, 2.1.190–91)

Group B: Words That Identify Places, Locations, and Parts

B.1. *DESERT.* When "desert" refers to a place, it means "wilderness," "uninhabited place," or "uncivilized place." Orlando begins one of the poems that he writes in the Forest of Arden with the following lines:

> Why should this a desert be?
>   For it is unpeopled? No.
> Tongues I'll hang on every tree
>   That shall civil sayings show. . . .
>
> (*As You Like It,* 3.2.119–22)

B.2. *CLOSET.* "Closet" sometimes means "private chamber," "private sitting room," or "study." Polonius says to the King, concerning Hamlet:

> My lord, he's going to his mother's closet.
> Behind the arras I'll convey myself
> To hear the process.
>
> (*Hamlet,* 3.3.27–29)

B.3. *GARDEN* and *ORCHARD.* For most Americans, the word "garden" refers to a plot of land set aside for the growing of vegetables or flowers. In Shakespeare's plays, however, the word "garden" usually refers to an area intended for recreation or relaxation, especially one where various plants are displayed. Isabella has such a place in mind when she says that Angelo "hath a garden circummured with brick, / Whose western side is with a vineyard backed . . ." (*Measure for Measure,* 4.1.27–28). "Orchard" may refer to such a garden or to a special part of one—a section containing herbs and fruit trees. When Benvolio says that Romeo "ran this way and leapt this orchard wall" (*Romeo and Juliet,* 2.1.5), he is referring to part of the wall around Capulet's garden, and Antony is referring to places for recreation when he tells the plebeians that Caesar has willed them:

> all his walks,
> His private arbors, and new-planted orchards,
> On this side Tiber. . . .
>
> (*Julius Caesar,* 3.2.247–49)

B.4. *FRONT.* "Front" may mean "forehead" or "foremost part" (and "to front" is thus "to front up to," "to oppose," "to confront"). "Front" may also mean "beginning," as it does when Florizel tells Perdita she is:

> no shepherdess, but Flora
> Peering in April's front.
>
> (*The Winter's Tale,* 4.4.2–3)

Group C: Words That Connect

● C.1. *BUT.* Probably no word in Shakespeare is more troublesome than the little word "but." It often has a meaning that we can best capture in the words "If it

were not true (that),'' ''If it is not true (that),'' or ''Were it not for the fact (that).''
One of these phrasings forms a suitable translation for each italicized ''but'' in
the following passages (the speakers are Edgar, Perdita, and Desdemona):

> World, world, O world!
> *But* that thy strange mutations make us hate thee,
> Life would not yield to age.
>
> (*King Lear*, 4.1.10–12)

> *But* that our feasts
> In every mess have folly, and the feeders
> Digest it with a custom, I should blush
> To see you so attired, swoon, I think,
> To show myself a glass.
>
> (*The Winter's Tale*, 4.4.10–14)

> and *but* my noble Moor
> Is true of mind, and made of no such baseness
> As jealous creatures are, it were enough
> To put him to ill thinking.
>
> (*Othello*, 3.4.26–29)

Furthermore, in order to make a strong affirmation, a Shakespearean character
may combine ''but'' with a negative, and translating the ''but'' in such a phras-
ing can be very difficult. For instance, in *Hamlet* (2.2.561-65), when Hamlet says:

> for it cannot be
> But I am pigeon-livered and lack gall
> To make oppression bitter, or ere this
> I should ha' fatted all the region kites
> With this slave's offal

he means, ''nothing can be true except that I am pigeon-livered'' or ''it is obvious that I am pigeon-livered.'' Othello uses ''but'' in a similar way in:

> I do not think but Desdemona's honest.
>
> (*Othello*, 3.3.225)

The line means, ''I do not have any thoughts at all except thoughts that Desdemona is honest'' or ''I do not think anything to be true except that Desdemona is honest.''

- C.2. *AN.* ''An'' frequently means ''if.'' Bianca says to Cassio:

> An you'll come to supper to-night, you may; an
> you will not, come when you are next prepared for.
>
> (*Othello*, 4.1.157–58)

And Sir Andrew tells Fabian:

> An't be any way, it must be with valor;
> for policy I hate.
>
> (*Twelfth Night*, 3.2.27–28)

C.3. *FOR.* ''For,'' sometimes in combination with ''that,'' often means ''because.'' Prospero reminds Ariel of the treatment Ariel received from the witch
Sycorax by saying:

And, for thou wast a spirit too delicate
To act her earthy and abhorred commands,
Refusing her grand hests, she did confine thee . . .
Into a cloven pine. . . .

(*The Tempest*, 1.2.272–74, 277)

And Edmund wonders why he should:

Stand in the plague of custom, and permit
The curiosity of nations to deprive me,
For that I am some twelve or fourteen moonshines
Lag of a brother?

(*King Lear*, 1.2.3–6)

• C.4. *OR*. Shakespeare regularly used "or . . . or" where we would use "either . . . or." Florizel says to Perdita:

Or I'll be thine, my fair,
Or not my father's. For I cannot be
Mine own, nor anything to any, if
I be not thine.

(*The Winter's Tale*, 4.4.42–45)

• C.5. *NOR*. Shakespeare regularly used "nor . . . nor" where we would use "neither . . . nor." "Nor night nor day no rest," says Leontes, complaining of his inability to sleep (*The Winter's Tale*, 2.3.1); and Olivia, wooing the disguised Viola, says:

I love thee so that, maugre all thy pride,
Nor wit nor reason can my passion hide.

(*Twelfth Night*, 3.1.148–49)

C.6. *ON*. "On" very often means "of." Concerning Mamillius's reaction to his mother's dishonor, Leontes says:

He straight declined, drooped, took it deeply,
Fastened and fixed the shame on't in himself. . . .

(*The Winter's Tale*, 2.3.14–15)

The Fool declares that Lear has:

banished two on's daughters, and did the
third a blessing against his will.

(*King Lear*, 1.4.97–98)

C.7. *THAT*. In Shakespeare's plays, "that" may have several meanings we do not expect it to have. It may mean "so that," "because," or "who," for example. "That" seems most oddly used, however, when a character who does not want to repeat a conjunction makes "that" a substitute for the conjunction. In the following passage, Desdemona uses each italicized "that" as a substitute for "if":

If e'er my will did trespass 'gainst his love
Either in discourse of thought or actual deed,
Or *that* mine eyes, mine ears, or any sense
Delighted them in any other form,
Or *that* I do not yet, and ever did,
And ever will (though he do shake me off
To beggarly divorcement) love him dearly,
Comfort forswear me!

(*Othello*, 4.2.152–59)

Group D: Words That Concern Love, Respect, Affection, and Illicit Desire

- D.1. FANCY. "Fancy" may mean "like," "love," or "desire." In *The Taming of the Shrew* Bianca responds to Kate's demand, "tell / Whom thou lov'st best" (2.1.8–9), by saying:

  > Believe me, sister, of all the men alive
  > I never yet beheld that special face
  > Which I could fancy more than any other.
  > (2.1.10–12)

- D.2. AFFECT. "Affect" often means "love," "like," "care for," "desire," or "strive for" (and "affection" may mean "disposition" or "inclination"). Kent uses "affect" in the sense of "care for" when he says, "I thought the King had more affected the Duke of Albany than Cornwall" (*King Lear*, 1.1.1–2), and in *The Taming of the Shrew*, Bianca uses "affect" to mean "love" or "desire" when she tells Kate:

  > If you affect him, sister, here I swear
  > I'll plead for you myself but you shall have him.
  > (2.1.14–15)

  D.3. FOND. "Fond" often means "foolish," "infatuated," or "doting." After he has suddenly become preoccupied with Isabella, Angelo says:

  > Ever till now,
  > When men were fond, I smiled and wondered how.
  > (*Measure for Measure*, 2.2.186–87)

  D.4. ADMIRE. "Admire" usually means "wonder at" or "be astonished by." Ferdinand therefore finds it appropriate that the young woman he considers "perfect" and "peerless" should have a name related to that word. "Admired Miranda!" he exclaims, when he learns what to call her:

  > Indeed the top of admiration, worth
  > What's dearest to the world!
  > (*The Tempest*, 3.1.38–39)

- D.5. KIND. "Kind" means, fundamentally, "true to one's nature, one's kind"; thus, "kind" may also mean "natural," "appropriate," and "proper." Furthermore, Shakespeare usually had his characters assume that human beings could be most significantly true to their natures by giving support and affection to members of their families, and therefore "kind," "unkind," and "kindless" are words that appear with considerable importance in reference to the giving or withholding of love in familial relationships. For example, because Claudius has killed his own brother, Hamlet calls him a "Remorseless, treacherous, lecherous, kindless villain!" (*Hamlet*, 2.2.566), and Lear asserts that:

  > . . . Gloucester's bastard son
  > Was kinder to his father than my daughters
  > Got 'tween the lawful sheets.
  > (*King Lear*, 4.6.113–15)

D.6. *NAUGHT.* "Naught" sometimes means, and "naughty" regularly means, "good for nothing," "very bad," "wicked," "vile," or "obscene," and, as a noun, "naught" may refer to illicit sexual activity. Oppressed by the fearful storm, the Fool tells the mad Lear, " 'tis a naughty night to swim in" (*King Lear*, 3.4.104–05), and Ophelia, after hearing some off-color remarks from Hamlet, responds:

> You are naught, you are naught. I'll mark the play.
> (*Hamlet*, 3.2.139)

● D.7. *BLOOD.* "Blood" may mean "passion," and it may refer to either sexual passion or anger. Othello means to refer to anger when he says, "My blood begins my safer guides to rule . . ." (*Othello*, 2.3.195), but Laertes means to refer to youthful erotic impulses when he tells Ophelia about her suitor:

> For Hamlet, and the trifling of his favor,
> Hold it a fashion and a toy in blood. . . .
> (*Hamlet*, 1.3.5–6)

D.8. *FOLLY.* "Folly" frequently refers to sexual folly. Sometimes it means "unchaste behavior," as when Othello says of Desdemona: "She turned to folly, and she was a whore" (*Othello*, 5.2.133). It may also refer to a rather harmless sexual license, as when Perdita says to Florizel:

> But that our feasts
> In every mess have folly, and the feeders
> Digest it with a custom, I should blush
> To see you so attired, swoon, I think,
> To show myself a glass.
> (*The Winter's Tale*, 4.4.10–14)

D.9. *WANTON.* "Wanton" refers to unrestrained behavior. It may mean "amorous," "lascivious," "lewd," "perverse," "contrary," or simply "sportive"; it may also mean "sport with" or "play with in an affectionate manner." Gloucester uses "wanton" to refer to offensively careless figures when he says, "As flies to wanton boys are we to th' gods; / They kill us for their sport" (*King Lear*, 4.1.36–37). In *The Winter's Tale*, however, after the young prince refuses to play with her, one of the Queen's ladies uses "wanton" to mean "sport with affectionately":

> We shall
> Present our services to a fine new prince
> One of these days, and then you'ld wanton with us,
> If we would have you.
> (2.1.16–19)

Group E: Words That Concern Growth and Well-being

E.1. *QUICK.* "Quick" may mean "living," "alive," "lively," "sprightly," "quick witted," and it also may mean "with child" (thus, "quicken" may mean "give life to"). Diana says to the King in *All's Well That Ends Well*:

Dead though she be, she feels her young one kick.
So there's my riddle: one that's dead is quick. . . .
                                        (5.3.299–300)

E.2. *SPEED.* "Speed" sometimes means "success," "welfare," "prosperity," or "fortune," and the word may also mean "helper." "To speed," then, may mean "to help" or "to cause to prosper." The servant in *The Winter's Tale* reports the death of Mamillius by saying:

The prince your son, with mere conceit and fear
Of the queen's speed, is gone.
                                        (3.2.142–43)

Group F: Words That Concern Perception, Testing, Reasoning, and Judgment

F.1. *CONCEIVE.* "Conceive" means both "understand" and "become pregnant." In the opening scene of *King Lear*, after Kent uses "conceive" to mean "understand," Gloucester immediately calls to mind the second meaning. The subject of their dialogue is Edmund, Gloucester's illegitimate son:

GLOUCESTER

I have so often blushed to acknowledge
him that now I am brazed to't.

KENT

I cannot conceive you.

GLOUCESTER

Sir, this young fellow's mother could;
whereupon she grew round-wombed, and had
indeed, sir, a son for her cradle ere she
had a husband for her bed.
                                        (*King Lear*, 1.1.9–15)

F.2. *CONCEIT.* "Conceit" may mean "mental conception," "idea," "imagination," or "fanciful design." It may also mean "mental capacity," "faculty of conceiving," "intelligence," or "understanding." It may also refer to a fanciful or clever idea or device. In *Twelfth Night* (3.4.275–76), when Fabian says that Cesario is,

as horribly conceited of him, and pants and
looks pale, as if a bear were at his heels

he means that Cesario has a concept of Andrew as horrifying as the concept Andrew has of Cesario.

F.3. *CENSURE.* "Censure" may mean "judgment" or "opinion" (rather than "condemnation"). Inviting the Queen and his mother to give their opinions before anyone is chosen to accompany Prince Edward from Ludlow, Richard says:

Madam, and you, my sister, will you go
To give your censures in this business?
                                        (*Richard III*, 2.2.143–44)

- F.4. *PROVE.* "Prove" may mean "test" or "try" (as in the popular saying, "The exception proves the rule"), and it also may mean "have experience of" or "find out by experience." Othello uses the word to mean "test" when he tells Iago:

> I'll see before I doubt; when I doubt, prove;
> And on the proof there is no more but this—
> Away at once with love or jealousy!
>
>   (*Othello*, 3.3.190–92)

F.5. *APPROVE.* "Approve" may mean "prove true," "confirm," "demonstrate," or "put to the test." It means "prove true" when Demetrius says of Antony:

>   I am full sorry
> That he approves the common liar, who
> Thus speaks of him at Rome. . . .
>
>   (*Antony and Cleopatra*, 1.1.59–61)

In *A Midsummer Night's Dream*, "approve" means "put to the test" when Puck says:

> Through the forest have I gone,
> But Athenian found I none
> On whose eyes I might approve
> This flower's force in stirring love.
>
>   (2.2.66–69)

F.6. *REGARD.* "Regard" may mean "look," "glance," "view," or "attention." It may also mean "consideration," as in the following lines, where Hamlet deplores the effects of thinking about the state we face after death:

> Thus conscience does make cowards of us all,
> And thus the native hue of resolution
> Is sicklied o'er with the pale cast of thought,
> And enterprises of great pitch and moment
> With this regard their currents turn awry
> And lose the name of action.
>
>   (*Hamlet*, 3.1.83–88)

F.7. *CONSCIENCE.* "Conscience" may refer to a person's moral faculty. So it does when Hamlet says, "The play's the thing / Wherein I'll catch the conscience of the king" (*Hamlet*, 2.2.590–91). Sometimes, however, "conscience" means "consciousness" or "reflection," as it does in the line quoted in the preceding paragraph:

> Thus conscience does make cowards of us all. . . .

Here Hamlet is referring to the human ability to consider the future and be frightened by its possibilities.

F.8. *URGE.* "Urge" may mean "suggest," "propose," "bring up," or "put forward in argument." The First Murderer asks Clarence:

> How canst thou urge God's dreadful law to us
> When thou hast broke it in such dear degree?
>
>   (*Richard III*, 1.4.204–5)

Group G: Words That Concern Chance and Probability

G.1. *ACCIDENT*. "Accident" often means "chance occurrence" or "incident." Perdita, who is frightened by the possibility of the King's rage, tells Florizel:

> Even now I tremble
> To think your father, by some accident,
> Should pass this way as you did.
>
> (*The Winter's Tale*, 4.4.18–20)

G.2. *HAPPILY*. The word "hap" means "fortune" or "chance." Thus "haply" means "by chance" or "perhaps," and "happily" may have those meanings, too. After Feste, disguised as Sir Topas, asks the imprisoned Malvolio, "What is the opinion of Pythagoras concerning wild fowl?" (*Twelfth Night*, 4.2.49–50), Malvolio dutifully replies:

> That the soul of our grandam might happily
> inhabit a bird.
>
> (4.2.51–52)

Group H: Words That Concern Food and Eating

H.1. *MEAT*. "Meat" commonly means "food." It may refer to food in general, but usually it refers to food prepared for humans—often, to food prepared by cooking. When Iago says to Desdemona, "The messengers of Venice stay the meat" (*Othello*, 4.2.170), he means that the messengers are waiting to eat their food for supper. When Cleopatra tells Proculeius that she will destroy herself rather than remain a prisoner to Octavius, she also uses "meat" to mean "food":

> Sir, I will eat no meat, I'll not drink, sir—
> If idle talk will once be necessary—
> I'll not sleep neither. This mortal house I'll ruin,
> Do Caesar what he can.
>
> (*Antony and Cleopatra*, 5.2.49–52)

Also, Cassius probably intends "meat" to mean "food" (rather than "animal flesh used for food") when he asks Brutus, "Upon what meat doth this our Caesar feed / That he is grown so great?" (*Julius Caesar*, 1.2.149–50).

H.2. *DIET*. "Diet" may mean "meals," "regimen," or "way of life," and it may also mean "restrict," "prescribe a diet for," or "feed." It has the last of these meanings when Iago says of Desdemona:

> Now I do love her too;
> Not out of absolute lust . . .
> But partly led to diet my revenge,
> For that I do suspect the lusty Moor
> Hath leaped into my seat. . . .
>
> (*Othello*, 2.1.285–86, 288–90)

H.3. *STOMACH.* "Stomach" may mean "appetite." It also may mean "anger," "arrogance," "courage," and "high spirit," and "to stomach" is sometimes "to resent." Lady Percy uses the word to mean "appetite" when she says to her husband:

> Tell me, sweet lord, what is't that takes from thee
> Thy stomach, pleasure, and thy golden sleep?
> (*1 Henry IV*, 2.3.37–38)

Group I: Words That Concern Quantity and Degree

I.1. *SOMETHING.* "Something" may mean "somewhat." Speaking of Ferdinand, Prospero says to Miranda:

> This gallant which thou seest
> Was in the wrack; and, but he's something stained
> With grief (that's beauty's canker), thou mightst call him
> A goodly person.
> (*The Tempest*, 1.2.414–17)

● I.2. *MERE.* "Mere" often means "absolute," "entire," "utter," "unmixed," or "unqualified." Malcolm, speaking of the King of England, says:

> how he solicits heaven
> Himself best knows, but strangely-visited people,
> All swol'n and ulcerous, pitiful to the eye,
> The mere despair of surgery, he cures. . . .
> (*Macbeth*, 4.3.149–52)

I.3. *ALL.* "All" may mean "altogether," "exclusively," or "entirely." Cordelia says:

> Sure I shall never marry like my sisters,
> [To love my father all.]
> (*King Lear*, 1.1.103–4)

Richard says he would like to make peace with Rivers and Dorset,

> That, all without desert, have frowned on me. . . .
> (*Richard III*, 2.1.68)

I.4. *EVEN.* "Even" often means "equal," "exactly," "quite," "equitable," "steadfast," or "uniform." The Gardener in *Richard II* uses it to mean "equal" when he says to a servant:

> Go thou and, like an executioner,
> Cut off the heads of too-fast-growing sprays
> That look too lofty in our commonwealth.
> All must be even in our government.
> (3.4.33–36)

Brutus uses it to mean "steadfast" when he rejects the idea of having an oath among the conspirators:

> but do not stain
> The even virtue of our enterprise,
> Nor th' insuppressive mettle of our spirits,
> To think that or our cause or our performance
> Did need an oath. . . .
>
> *(Julius Caesar,* 2.1.132–36)

I.5. *HOME.* "Home" may mean "to the intended destination," "to a finish," "thoroughly," or "to the point." Enraged by his treatment by Goneril and Regan, Lear declares:

> But I will punish home.
> No, I will weep no more.
>
> *(King Lear,* 3.4.16–17)

He means, of course, "punish thoroughly."

I.6. *JUST.* "Just" may mean "exact," and "justly" may mean "exactly," "properly," "truthfully," "deservedly," or "with good reason." After Romeo kills Tybalt, Juliet attacks him as:

> Just opposite to what thou justly seem'st—
> A damnèd saint, an honorable villain!
>
> *(Romeo and Juliet,* 3.2.78–79)

I.7. *PREGNANT.* "Pregnant" indicates some kind of fullness or readiness, and it may mean "clever," "resourceful," "compelling," "evident," "obvious," or "ready." Viola uses "pregnant" when thinking about the devil, who is a resourceful and ready liar:

> Disguise, I see thou art a wickedness
> Wherein the pregnant enemy does much.
>
> *(Twelfth Night,* 2.2.26–27)

Iago uses "pregnant" to refer to a conclusion that he wants Roderigo to consider compelling:

> Now, sir, this granted—as it is a
> most pregnant and unforced position—who stands so
> eminent in the degree of this fortune as Cassio does?
>
> *(Othello,* 2.1.232–34)

Edgar uses "pregnant to" to mean "susceptible to" or "ready for" when he tells Gloucester he is:

> A most poor man, made tame to fortune's blows,
> Who, by the art of known and feeling sorrows,
> Am pregnant to good pity.
>
> *(King Lear,* 4.6.217–19)

Hamlet, however, uses "pregnant" in the sense of "filled" or "animated" as he accuses himself of not vigorously pursuing revenge on his father's killer. He mopes, he says, "Like John-a-dreams, unpregnant of my cause . . ." *(Hamlet,* 2.2.553).

Group J: Words That Negate

J.1. *NEVER.* "Never" sometimes means "not." Comparing himself with several gods who became inferior creatures in order to pursue mortal women, Florizel says:

> Their transformations
> Were never for a piece of beauty rarer,
> Nor in a way so chaste. . . .
> (*The Winter's Tale*, 4.4.31–33)

J.2. *NOTHING.* "Nothing" may mean "not at all," "not," or "by no means." Brutus says to Cassius:

> That you do love me I am nothing jealous.
> (*Julius Caesar*, 1.2.162)

Group K: Words That Identify Approved Effects, Qualities, and Attitudes

K.1. *PROPER.* "Proper" may mean "handsome" or "fine" (for additional meanings, see Q.2). Desdemona describes Lodovico as "a proper man" (*Othello*, 4.3.35), and Viola laments:

> How easy is it for the proper false
> In women's waxen hearts to set their forms!
> (*Twelfth Night*, 2.2.28–29)

● K.2. *BRAVE.* "Brave" often means "fine," "splendid," or "grand." The inexperienced Miranda says:

> How beauteous mankind is! O brave new world
> That has such people in't!
> (*The Tempest*, 5.1.183–84)

K.3. *TALL.* "Tall" frequently means "strong," "sturdy," or "spirited." Thus, defending his sponsorship of Sir Andrew as a wooer for Olivia, Toby tells Maria that:

> He's as tall a man as any's in Illyria.
> (*Twelfth Night*, 1.3.18)

● K.4. *LIKE.* "Like" may mean "please." At the end of *As You Like It*, the boy actor who has been playing Rosalind says in the Epilogue:

> If I were a woman, I would kiss as many of you
> as had beards that pleased me, complexions that
> liked me, and breaths that I defied not. . . .
> (lines 16–18)

K.5. *TRUE.* "True" may mean "honest," "trustworthy," or "reliable." Casca, speaking of the reaction of the commoners to Caesar, says:

If the tag-rag people did not clap him
and hiss him, according as he pleased and
displeased them, as they use to do the
players in the theatre, I am no true man.

(Julius Caesar, 1.2.256–59)

K.6. *MEET.* "Meet" sometimes means "fitting" or "proper." The disguised Kent
says to Cordelia:

My boon I make it that you know me not
Till time and I think meet.

(King Lear, 4.7.10–11)

• K.7. *SAD.* "Sad" often means "serious," "sober," or "grave" (rather than
"glum" or "morose"). When Olivia says that Malvolio

is sad and civil,
And suits well for a servant with my fortunes

she means he is serious and sedate *(Twelfth Night, 3.4.4–5)*.

K.8. *REMORSE.* "Remorse" usually means "compassion" or "pity." Promising
his support to the supposedly wronged Othello, Iago says:

Let him command,
And to obey shall be in me remorse,
What bloody business ever.

(Othello, 3.3.467–69)

• K.9. *HONEST.* "Honest" may mean "honorable" or "respectable"; a speaker
who is referring to a man is more likely to have one of those meanings in mind
than is a speaker who is referring to a woman. Thus, Othello uses "honest" to
mean "honorable" when he says of Iago:

An honest man he is, and hates the slime
That sticks on filthy deeds.

(Othello, 5.2.148–49)

"Honest" may also mean "not guilty of illicit sexual behavior," and "honesty"
may mean "chastity" or "purity." These meanings usually occur when speakers
are referring to women rather than to men. Such are the meanings that Hamlet
intends when he tells Ophelia that, if she is "honest and fair," then her honesty
"should admit no discourse" to her beauty; "for the power of beauty," he explains,

will sooner
transform honesty from what it is to a bawd than the
force of honesty can translate beauty into his likeness.

(Hamlet, 3.1.107–8, 111–13)

K.10. *PATIENCE.* "Patience" may mean "composure while beset by difficulties" or "calmness while suffering misfortunes." Resolving to endure a storm
that he thinks to be in sympathy with his hostile daughters, Lear declares, "I
will be the pattern of all patience; / I will say nothing" *(King Lear, 3.2.37–38)*.
Worcester, as he stands before his enemy expecting a sentence of death says:

What I have done my safety urged me to;
And I embrace this fortune patiently,
Since not to be avoided it falls on me.

(1 Henry IV, 5.5.11–13)

Group L: Words That Identify Unpleasant Attitudes, Qualities, States, Effects, and Objects

● L.1. *JEALOUS.* "Jealous" may mean "suspiciously careful," "watchful," "apprehensive of evil," or "doubtful," and "jealousy" may mean "suspicion" or "mistrust." In *Julius Caesar* (1.2.71), when Cassius says,

And be not jealous on me, gentle Brutus

he means, "be not suspicious of me."

L.2. *SECURE.* "Secure" may mean simply "safe" or "free from care," but it may also mean "over confident," "heedless," "unsuspecting," or "careless." In *Othello* (3.3.198), when Iago tells Othello,

Wear your eyes thus, not jealous nor secure . . .

he is advising his general to be prudently alert: not full of suspicion and also not foolishly free from concern.

L.3. *NICE.* "Nice" usually means "overly precise," "finical," "squeamish," "prudish," "minutely accurate," "delicate," "overly subtle," "pampered," or "coy" (it may also mean "trivial"). Buckingham tells Richard that his refusal to accept the crown:

argues conscience in your grace,
But the respects thereof are nice and trivial. . . .

(Richard III, 3.7.174–75)

● L.4. *DOUBT.* "Doubt" often means "fear." When Cassio expresses concern that Othello will forget him and appoint another to his office, Desdemona reassures him by saying:

Do not doubt that; before Emilia here
I give thee warrant of thy place.

(Othello, 3.3.19–20)

Also, "doubt" may sometimes mean "suspect." Says Hamlet:

My father's spirit—in arms? All is not well.
I doubt some foul play.

(Hamlet, 1.2.255–56)

L.5. *FEAR.* Occasionally, Shakespearean characters use "fear" with the meaning, "be anxious about" or "be afraid for." Thus, Othello tells Iago, "Fear not my government" (*Othello*, 3.3.256). "Fear" may also mean "worry about" or "distrust," as it does when Edmund tells Regan, "Fear me not" (*King Lear*, 5.1.16). In addition, "fear" may mean "frighten," and, as a noun, it may mean "object of fear." It has the former meaning when Antony says, "Thou canst not fear us, Pompey, with thy sails" (*Antony and Cleopatra*, 2.6.24), and it has the latter meaning when Theseus tells Hippolyta:

> Such tricks hath strong imagination
> That, if it would but apprehend some joy,
> It comprehends some bringer of that joy;
> Or in the night, imagining some fear,
> How easy is a bush supposed a bear!
>
> (*A Midsummer Night's Dream*, 5.1.18–22)

- L.6. *HUMOR.* A "humor" is literally a moisture or fluid. Before Shakespeare's day, authorities had come to use the word "humors" to refer to four bodily fluids (blood, choler, melancholy, and phlegm) that they believed important in the formation of a person's physical characteristics and emotional qualities. Later, "humor" took on the meanings "temperament," "disposition," "caprice," "temporary state of mind," and "fancy." "Humorous" thus came to mean not only "damp," but also "capricious" and "eccentric." Benvolio plays on both meanings of "humorous" when he says, of Romeo:

> he hath hid himself among these trees
> To be consorted with the humorous night.
>
> (*Romeo and Juliet*, 2.1.30–31)

Further, "humor" may mean "cajole," "win by flattery", "play on (someone's) eccentricities." So Cassius says, "If I were Brutus now and he were Cassius, / He should not humor me" (*Julius Caesar*, 1.2.311–12).

L.7. *FOUL.* "Foul" may mean "ugly" or "unattractive." The Chorus in *Henry V* says that the French, being eager for battle:

> Do the low-rated English play at dice;
> And chide the cripple tardy-gaited night
> Who like a foul and ugly witch doth limp
> So tediously away.
>
> (4. Chorus. 19–22)

L.8. *FEARFUL.* "Fearful" may mean "full of fear" or "timid," but it also may mean "dreadful" or "terrible," as in Clarence's first speech to the Keeper:

> O, I have passed a miserable night,
> So full of fearful dreams, of ugly sights,
> That, as I am a Christian faithful man,
> I would not spend another such a night
> Though 'twere to buy a world of happy days. . . .
>
> (*Richard III*, 1.4.2–6)

L.9. *IDLE.* "Idle" usually means "silly," "foolish," "useless," or "trifling." After Romeo tells him that he talks of nothing, Mercutio replies:

> True, I talk of dreams;
> Which are the children of an idle brain,
> Begot of nothing but vain fantasy. . . .
>
> (*Romeo and Juliet*, 1.4.96–98)

L.10. *PEEVISH.* "Peevish" usually means "silly," "fretful," or "obstinate." After he is unable to calm his daughter, who is weeping because her husband, Mortimer, is about to depart, Glendower says:

> She is desperate here. A peevish self-willed harlotry,
> One that no persuasion can do good upon.
> > > (*1 Henry IV,* 3.1.196–97)

L.11. *SHREWD.* "Shrewd" frequently means "petulant," "biting," "harsh," "hard," "evil," or "unpleasant." Hortensio describes Kate, the so-called shrew, as:

> > > intolerable curst,
> And shrewd and froward. . . .
> > > (*The Taming of the Shrew,* 1.2.87–88)

L.12. *CURST.* "Curst" usually means "ill-tempered," "cross," or "malignant" (not "oppressed with a curse"). Petruchio says that Katherine is sometimes called:

> > > plain Kate,
> And bonny Kate, and sometimes Kate the curst.
> > > (*The Taming of the Shrew,* 2.1.185–86)

L.13. *FELL.* "Fell" may mean "cruel," "fierce," or "deadly." Thus, Lady Macbeth asks the "spirits / That tend on mortal thoughts" to "unsex" her and to "Stop up th' access and passage to remorse,"

> That no compunctious visitings of nature
> Shake my fell purpose nor keep peace between
> Th' effect and it.
> > > (*Macbeth,* 1.5.38–39, 42–45)

Group M: Words That Concern Dangerous Attitudes, Harmful Activities, Injurious Behavior, and Feared Conditions

M.1. *CONFUSION.* "Confusion" may mean "destruction" or "utter ruin." In *A Midsummer Night's Dream,* Lysander, lamenting the fate of true love, says:

> > > ere a man hath power to say "Behold!"
> The jaws of darkness do devour it up:
> So quick bright things come to confusion.
> > > (1.1.147–49)

M.2. *CONFOUND.* As "confusion" may mean "destruction," so "confound" may mean "destroy" or "waste." Antony says to Cleopatra:

> Now for the love of Love and her soft hours,
> Let's not confound the time with conference harsh.
> > > (*Antony and Cleopatra,* 1.1.44–45)

M.3. *PRACTICE.* "Practice" may mean "plot," "scheme," or "strategy." Olivia is speaking of the plot Malvolio has suffered when she says:

> This practice hath most shrewdly passed upon thee. . . .
> *(Twelfth Night,* 5.1.342)

• M.4. *MISCHIEF.* "Mischief" usually means "calamity," "harm," "injury," or "evil deed" (and not "irritating behavior"). Orsino is planning to kill Cesario (Viola) when he says:

> My thoughts are ripe in mischief.
> I'll sacrifice the lamb that I do love
> To spite a raven's heart within a dove.
> *(Twelfth Night,* 5.1.123–25)

M.5. *SUGGESTION.* "Suggestion" may mean simply "prompting," but it may also mean "temptation" or "prompting to evil." Blunt promises the rebel Hotspur that he shall have:

> pardon absolute for yourself and these
> Herein misled by your suggestion.
> *(1 Henry IV,* 4.3.50–51)

• M.6. *ABUSE.* "Abuse" often means "deceive," "betray," "cheat," or "impose upon." It may also mean "slander" or "disgrace." Antigonus means "deceived" when he says that Leontes is,

> abused and by some putter-on
> That will be damned for't.
> *(The Winter's Tale,* 2.1.141–42)

Iago, however, means "slander" when he says:

> I'll have our Michael Cassio on the hip,
> Abuse him to the Moor in the rank garb. . . .
> *(Othello,* 2.1.299–300)

M.7. *ANNOY.* "Annoy" may mean "pain" or "grief." It may also mean "harm" or "injury," and "to annoy" is "to hurt" or "to molest." Before the murder of Caesar, Cassius warns that Antony is a "shrewd contriver" and that:

> his means,
> If he improve them, may well stretch so far
> As to annoy us all. . . .
> *(Julius Caesar,* 2.1.158–60)

M.8. *CROSS.* "Cross" may mean "frustration," "difficulty," "trouble," "contradiction," and "to cross" may mean "to vex," "annoy," "frustrate," "prevent," or "thwart." York laments:

> Comfort's in heaven, and we are on the earth,
> Where nothing lives but crosses, cares and grief.
> *(Richard II,* 2.2.78–79)

● M.9. *ENVY.* "Envy" frequently means "malice," "ill-will," or "enmity." Thus, Romeo, not wanting to be parted from Juliet, says, "Look, love, what envious streaks / Do lace the severing clouds in yonder East" (*Romeo and Juliet*, 3.5.7–8), and Antony, in praising Brutus, says that:

> All the conspirators save only he
> Did that they did in envy of great Caesar. . . .
>
> (*Julius Caesar*, 5.5.69–70)

Group N: Words That Identify Unattractive Persons and Trivial Things and Events

N.1. *NATURAL.* "Natural" may mean "born fool," "idiot," or "halfwit." After Caliban shows an absurd respect for the drunken butler, Stephano, Trinculo comments:

> "Lord" quoth he? That a monster should be
> such a natural!
>
> (*The Tempest*, 3.2.31–32)

N.2. *COMPANION.* "Companion" sometimes means "base fellow" or "knave." King Henry instructs his lords to inquire about his son:

> at London, 'mongst the taverns there,
> For there, they say, he daily doth frequent,
> With unrestrainèd loose companions. . . .
>
> (*Richard II*, 5.3.5–7)

● N.3. *TOY.* "Toy" usually means "trifle," "whim," or "idle fancy." Othello tells the Duke and senators that he will not be drawn from his military duties by the "light-winged toys / Of feathered Cupid" (*Othello*, 1.3.268–69), and after the murder of Duncan, Macbeth says:

> from this instant
> There's nothing serious in mortality:
> All is but toys.
>
> (*Macbeth*, 2.3.88–90)

Group O: Words That Concern Permission and Prevention

O.1. *LET.* "Let" may mean "hinder" or "impede," and, as a noun, it may mean "obstacle." Hamlet means "hinder" when he commands his fellows to leave him free to follow the apparition:

> Unhand me, gentlemen.
> By heaven, I'll make a ghost of him that lets me!
> I say, away!
>
> (*Hamlet*, 1.4.84–86)

O.2. *DEFEND*. "Defend" sometimes means "forbid." Mowbray uses it in both that and its more expected sense when he says:

> My name is Thomas Mowbray, Duke of Norfolk,
> Who hither come engagèd by my oath
> (Which God defend a knight should violate!)
> Both to defend my loyalty and truth
> To God, my king, and my succeeding issue
> Against the Duke of Hereford that appeals me. . . .
>
> (*Richard II*, 1.3.16–21)

O.3. *ALLOW*. "Allow" may mean "approve" or "sanction." It may also mean "admit," "concede," or "grant." Lear uses it to mean "approve" when he says to the heavens:

> If you do love old men, if your sweet sway
> Allow obedience, if you yourselves are old,
> Make it your cause.
>
> (*King Lear*, 2.4.185–87)

Group P: Words That Concern Social Activities and Interactions

● P.1. *PART*. "Part" may mean "action," "deed," "accomplishment," or "personal quality." Desdemona says to the Duke and senators:

> I saw Othello's visage in his mind,
> And to his honors and his valiant parts
> Did I my soul and fortunes consecrate.
>
> (*Othello*, 1.3.252–54)

Cleopatra, describing the attitude Antony professed to have toward her, says:

> Eternity was in our lips and eyes,
> Bliss in our brows' bent: none our parts so poor
> But was a race of heaven.
>
> (*Antony and Cleopatra*, 1.3.35–37)

P.2. *UNDERTAKE*. "Undertake" may mean "assume," "take in charge," "take on," "take up a matter for," or "have to do with." It means "take on" or "take in charge" when Goneril says of Albany:

> It is the cowish terror of his spirit,
> That dares not undertake. He'll not feel wrongs
> Which tie him to an answer.
>
> (*King Lear*, 4.2.12–14)

P.3. *OFFICE*. "Office" often means "action," "proper function," or "service." Malcolm uses it to mean "action" or "service" when he says:

> To show an unfelt sorrow is an office
> Which the false man does easy.
>
> (*Macbeth*, 2.3.132–33)

Rosalind uses it to mean "proper function" when she says to Celia:

Nay, now thou goest from Fortune's office to
Nature's.
(As You Like It, 1.2.38–39)

P.4. *CHARGE.* "Charge" may mean "burden" or "command," and it may also mean "duty" or "expense." Macbeth says to Macduff:

Of all men else I have avoided thee.
But get thee back! My soul is too much charged
With blood of thine already.
(Macbeth, 5.8.4–6)

P.5. *SYMPATHY.* "Sympathy" means "agreement," "correspondence," or "harmony." In *A Midsummer Night's Dream,* Lysander gives a melancholy assessment of the fates of true lovers by saying:

if there were a sympathy in choice,
War, death, or sickness did lay siege to it. . . .
(1.1.141–42)

P.6. *QUIT.* "Quit" may mean "acquit," "pay for," "pay off," "repay," "reward," or "release." The blinded Gloucester means "repay" when he says:

Edmund, enkindle all the sparks of nature
To quit this horrid act.
(King Lear, 3.7.86–87)

P.7. *TRICK.* "Trick" may mean "peculiar habit" or "characteristic expression." The blinded Gloucester recognizes Lear by the "trick" of his voice *(King Lear,* 4.6. 105), and Cleopatra says to Dolabella:

You laugh when boys or women tell their dreams;
Is't not your trick?
(Antony and Cleopatra, 5.2.74–75)

Group Q: Words That Concern Social Position, Social Relations, and Possession

Q.1. *GENTLE.* "Gentle" may mean "of gentle birth," "well-born," "noble." When York says that King Richard "with . . . gentle sorrow" shook off dirt thrown on his head *(Richard II,* 5.2.31), he means "noble sorrow," and Richard of Gloucester intends "gentle" to mean "of noble birth" when he complains:

Since every Jack became a gentleman,
There's many a gentle person made a Jack.
(Richard III, 1.3.71–72)

Q.2. *PROPER.* "Proper" may mean "belonging distinctly to," "peculiar," "appropriate to," "characteristic of," or "own" (for another important meaning, see K.1). In *The Winter's Tale,* (2.3.139–40), when Leontes threatens the child, Perdita, by saying,

> The bastard brains with these my proper hands
> Shall I dash out

he means "my own hands."

● Q.3. *OWE.* "Owe" may mean "be indebted to," but it often means "own," "possess," or "have." Ferdinand says of the song played by Ariel:

> The ditty does remember my drowned father.
> This is no mortal business, nor no sound
> That the earth owes. I hear it now above me.
> > (*The Tempest,* 1.2.406–8)

Malcolm says of the executed Cawdor:

> > He died
> As one that had been studied in his death
> To throw away the dearest thing he owed
> As 'twere a careless trifle.
> > (*Macbeth,* 1.4.8–11)

Q.4. *ADDITION.* "Addition" may mean "mark of distinction," "title," or "honors." Lear tells Cornwall and Albany that he intends to make them rulers:

> > Only we shall retain
> The name, and all th' addition to a king. The sway,
> Revenue, execution of the rest,
> Belovèd sons, be yours. . . .
> > (*King Lear,* 1.1.135–38)

● Q.5. *GRACE.* "Grace" may mean "adorn" or "do honor to." It may also mean "favor," "beneficent virtue," or "sense of duty." It may also refer to spiritual grace or the grace said before meals, and it may be a form of address, meaning "highness." Furthermore, "gracious" may mean "righteous," "attractive," or "honored." Falstaff plays on three meanings of "grace" in the following exchange with Prince Hal:

FALSTAFF

And I prithee, sweet wag, when thou art a
king, as, God save thy grace—majesty I
should say, for grace thou wilt have none—

PRINCE

What, none?

FALSTAFF
No, by my troth; not so much as will serve
to be prologue to an egg and butter.
> > (*1 Henry IV,* 1.2.14–19)

Group R: Words That Concern Openness, Revelation, and Secrecy

R.1. *ROUND*. "Round" may mean "plain," "honest," "outspoken," "blunt," or "unceremonious." Othello informs the senators and Duke:

I will a round unvarnished tale deliver
Of my whole course of love. . . .

(*Othello*, 1.3.90–91)

R.2. *CLOSE*. "Close" may mean "secret," "in concealment," or "in hiding." Richard asks the Page:

Know'st thou not any whom corrupting gold
Will tempt unto a close exploit of death?

(*Richard III*, 4.2.34–35)

In *A Midsummer Night's Dream*, Oberon instructs Puck:

Stand close. This is the same Athenian.

(3.2.41)

• R.3. *DISCOVER*. "Discover" usually means "reveal," "make known," or "display." Autolycus, disguised as a courtier, demands that the Clown and Shepherd provide him information about their business at the court:

Your affairs there, what, with whom, the
condition of that fardel, the place of your dwelling,
your names, your ages, of what having, breeding, and
anything that is fitting to be known, discover.

(*The Winter's Tale*, 4.4.705–8)

Group S: Words That Assist

• S.1. *WILL* and *WOULD*. In Shakespeare's plays, several verbs that assist other verbs create difficulties for modern readers. Among these are "will" and "would." Both frequently express a willing of some sort—a wish, inclination, or intention. For example:

When Hamlet says that the idea of killing Claudius at prayer "would be scanned" (*Hamlet*, 3.3.75), he means "demands to be scanned."

When Hamlet speaks of a politician "that would circumvent God" (*Hamlet*, 5.1.75), he means one who "wished to circumvent."

When Macbeth says that in Banquo's nature "reigns that / Which would be feared" (*Macbeth*, 3.1.50–51), he means "demands to be feared."

When Othello says, "If heaven would make me such another world" (*Othello*, 5.2.145), he means "If heaven were disposed to make."

When Cleopatra says that Antony "would shine on those / That make their looks by his . . ." (*Antony and Cleopatra*, 1.5.55–56), her "would" means "wished to."

When Sebastian says to Toby, "I will be free from thee" (*Twelfth Night*, 4.1.37), he means essentially, "I wish to be free" or "I am determined to be free," not "I am going to be free."

When Olivia says, "Give us the place alone; we will hear this divinity" (*Twelfth Night*, 1.5.207), she means, "we wish to hear."

In addition, "would" and "will" may describe actions that are habitual, customary, or inevitable. Thus:

When Hamlet says, "Foul deeds will rise, / Though all the earth o'erwhelm them, to men's eyes" (*Hamlet*, 1.2.257–58), he means "will inevitably rise."

When Othello says, "This to hear / Would Desdemona seriously incline . . ." (*Othello*, 1.3. 145–46), he means, "did over and over incline."

S.2. *SHALL* and *SHOULD*. "Shall" and "should" can also create difficulties for modern readers. First, either one may suggest inevitability. The following passages, spoken by Othello, Antony, and Octavius, provide examples:

> If I once stir
> Or do but lift this arm, the best of you
> Shall sink in my rebuke.
>
> (*Othello*, 2.3.197–99)

> Egypt, thou knew'st too well
> My heart was to thy rudder tied by th' strings,
> And thou shouldst tow me after.
>
> (*Antony and Cleopatra*, 3.11.56–58)

> But you are come
> A market-maid to Rome, and have prevented
> The ostentation of our love; which, left unshown,
> Is often left unloved. We should have met you
> By sea and land, supplying every stage
> With an augmented greeting.
>
> (*Antony and Cleopatra*, 3.6.50–55)

In the first passage, Othello means "shall inevitably sink"—"shall sink without question." In the second, Antony means "would inevitably tow." And in the third, Octavius means, "would certainly have met you."

In addition, "should" can refer to the time to come, and when it does, it means "was to" (that is, "was to in the future"). For example:

When Romeo says, "I think / He told me Paris should have married Juliet" (*Romeo and Juliet*, 5.3.77–78), he means "was to have married Juliet."

When Juliet says, "I do remember well where I should be, / And there I am" (*Romeo and Juliet*, 5.3.149–50) she means, "where I was to be."

S.3. *HAD*. Still another auxiliary that can cause difficulties is "had." In Shakespeare's plays, "had" often refers to something that did not actually occur. The translation that most often fits in those instances is "would have." For example:

When King Henry says, "Had I so lavish of my presence been . . . / Opinion, that did help me to the crown, / Had still kept loyal to possession . . ." (*1 Henry IV*, 3.2.39, 42–43), he means "opinion would have still kept loyal."

When Diana says of Bertram, "He had sworn to marry me / When his wife's dead . . ." (*All's Well That Ends Well*, 4.2.71–72), she means "would have sworn."

And when Othello threatens Iago by saying, "Thou hadst been better have been born a dog / Than answer my waked wrath!" (*Othello*, 3.3.362–63), he means "would have been better."

Group T: Words Related to Salvation and Religion

T.1. *REDEEM*. "Redeem" may mean "rescue" or "ransom." It may also mean "repay in full," "atone for," or "make up for." Lear says, over the corpse of his daughter, Cordelia:

This feather stirs; she lives! If it be so,
It is a chance which does redeem all sorrows
That ever I have felt.

(*King Lear*, 5.3.266–68)

T.2. *DIVINITY*. "Divinity" may mean "sacred discourse" or "theological reasoning." Iago has chiefly the latter meaning in mind when he says:

How am I then a villain
To counsel Cassio to this parallel course,
Directly to his good? Divinity of hell!
When devils will the blackest sins put on,
They do suggest at first with heavenly shows,
As I do now.

(*Othello*, 2.3.331–36)

WORKS CITED

Abbott, E. A. 1870. *A Shakespearian Grammar.* (3rd ed.). London: Macmillan.

Barber, Charles. 1976. *Early Modern English.* London: André Deutsch Limited.

Barnett, J. E. 1984. "Facilitating Retention through Instruction about Text Structure." *Journal of Reading Behavior* 16: 1–13.

Bennett, R. C. 1968/69. "Oral Tradition and the Teaching of Shakespeare." *English Language Teaching* 23: 56–59.

Blake, N. F. 1983. *Shakespeare's Language: An Introduction.* New York: St. Martin's.

Blinderman, Abraham. 1975/76. "I Actually Know Not Too Much on Shakespeare." *College English* 37: 353–57.

Brook, G. L. 1976. *The Language of Shakespeare.* London: André Deutsch Limited.

Carr, E., and K. Wixson. 1985/86. "Guidelines for Evaluating Vocabulary Instruction." *Journal of Reading* 29: 588–95.

Carter, Candy. 1983. "Move Over, Marva, or How 35 Students Learned 'To Be or Not To Be.'" *English Journal* 72 (3): 27–29.

Eastman, Richard M. 1982. "Is It Time to Translate Shakespeare?" *English Journal* 71 (3): 41–46.

Editorial. 1985. "Translating Shakespeare into English." *The Use of English* 36 (1): 2–6.

Feingold, Michael. 1984. "Alas! Poor Shakespeare." *Village Voice Literary Supplement,* June, 11.

Franz, Wilhelm. 1924. *Shakespeare-grammatik* (3rd ed.). Heidelberg: Winters.

Frey, Charles. 1984. "Teaching Shakespeare in America." *Shakespeare Quarterly* 35: 541–59.

Gilbert, Miriam. 1984. "Teaching Shakespeare through Performance." *Shakespeare Quarterly* 35: 601–8.

Hapke, Laura. 1984. "Deciphering Shakespeare: Some Practical Classroom Techniques." *The English Record* 35 (2): 11–12.

Harbage, Alfred. 1963. *William Shakespeare: A Reader's Guide.* New York: Farrar, Straus, and Giroux.

Harbage, Alfred. (ed.) 1969. *William Shakespeare: The Complete Works* (The Pelican Shakespeare). Baltimore: Penguin.

Hulme, Hilda. 1962. *Explorations in Shakespeare's Language: Some Problems of Lexical Meaning in the Dramatic Text.* London: Longmans.

Hulme, Hilda. 1972. *Yours That Read Him: An Introduction to Shakespeare's Language.* London: Ginn, for the Shakespeare Workshop.

Hussey, S. S. 1982. *The Literary Language of Shakespeare.* London: Longman.

Kernodle, George R. 1949. "Basic Problems in Reading Shakespeare." *Quarterly Journal of Speech* 35: 36–43.

McKenna, Michael. 1975/76. "Shakespeare in Grade 8." *Journal of Reading* 19: 205–7.

Marzano, R. J., R. S. Brandt, C. S. Hughes, B. F. Jones, B. Z. Presseisen, S. C. Rankin, and C. Suhor. 1988. *Dimensions of Thinking: A Framework for Curriculum and Instruction.* Alexandria, Va.: Association for Supervision and Curriculum Development.

Mayer, Richard E. 1984. "Aids to Text Comprehension." *Educational Psychologist* 19: 30–42.

Murray, James A.H., Henry Bradley, W.A. Craigie, and C. T. Onions. 1933. *Oxford English Dictionary.* Oxford: Oxford University Press. (Includes 12 volumes and supplement).

Nagy, William E. 1988. *Teaching Vocabulary to Improve Reading Comprehension.* Urbana: National Council of Teachers of English and International Reading Association. (In press).

O'Brien, Ellen J. 1984. "Inside Shakespeare: Using Performance Techniques to Achieve Traditional Goals." *Shakespeare Quarterly* 35: 621–31.

Omans, Stuart E. 1973. "Troublesome Words in Shakespeare's Plays." *Exercise Exchange* 18 (1): 13–17.

Onions, C. T. 1986. *A Shakespeare Glossary.* Rev. Robert D. Eagleson. Oxford: Clarendon Press.

Price, George R. 1962. *Reading Shakespeare's Plays.* Great Neck, N.Y.: Barron's Educational Series, Inc.

Richards, I. A. 1929. *Practical Criticism: A Study of Literary Judgment.* New York: Harcourt, Brace and World.

Renz, Ben. 1942. "Teaching Shakespeare." *English Journal* 31: 56–59.

Schmidt, Alexander. 1962. *Shakespeare-Lexicon.* 5th ed. Rev. Gregor I. Sarrazin. Berlin: Walter de Gruyter. (In two volumes).

Stahl, Steven A. 1985/86. "Three Principles of Effective Vocabulary Instruction." *Journal of Reading* 29: 662–68.

Swander, Homer. 1984. "In Our Time: Such Audiences We Wish Him." *Shakespeare Quarterly.* 35: 528–40.

Swander, Homer. 1985. "Teaching Shakespeare: Tradition and the Future." *In* John F. Andrews, ed., *William Shakespeare: His World, His Work, His Influence,* vol. 3: 873–87. New York: Scribner's.

Thorpe, Peter. 1967. "Riddling Confession Finds But Riddling Shrift." *Improving College and University Teaching* 15: 188.

Veidemanis, Gladys. 1964. "Shakespeare in the High School Classroom." *English Journal* 53: 240–47.

Wilson, F. P. 1941. "Shakespeare and the Diction of Common Life." *Proceedings of the British Academy* 27: 167–97.

AUTHOR

Randal Robinson is a Professor of English at Michigan State University. He regularly teaches courses in Shakespeare, Renaissance drama, forms of drama, and writing and is the author of *"Hamlet" in the 1950s: An Annotated Bibliography*. In recent years, he has provided workshops on the reading of Shakespeare for sophomores from three Michigan high schools and has organized and chaired workshops on the teaching of Shakespeare's language for NCTE and the Shakespeare Association of America. He contributes to workshops on the use of performance in teaching drama, and he has appeared in both university and community theater productions. He has served as acting director of writing programs and acting associate chair for undergraduate programs for his department.